10-MINUTE DECLUTTER

The Stress-Free Habit for Simplifying Your Home

Written by:

Barrie Davenport
liveboldandbloom.com

S.J. Scott
www.HabitBooks.com

Disclaimer

No part of this publication may be reproduced or transmitted in any form or by any means, mechanical or electronic, including photocopying or recording, or by any information storage and retrieval system, or transmitted by email without permission in writing from the publisher.

While all attempts have been made to verify the information provided in this publication, neither the author nor the publisher assumes any responsibility for errors, omissions or contrary interpretations of the subject matter herein.

This book is for entertainment purposes only. The views expressed are those of the author alone, and should not be taken as expert instruction or commands. The reader is responsible for his or her own actions.

Adherence to all applicable laws and regulations, including international, federal, state and local laws governing professional licensing, business practices, advertising and all other aspects of doing business in the US, Canada or any other jurisdiction is the sole responsibility of the purchaser or reader.

Neither the author nor the publisher assumes any responsibility or liability whatsoever on the behalf of the purchaser or reader of these materials.

Any perceived slight of any individual or organization is purely unintentional.

Your Free Gift (1)

As a way of saying *thanks* for your purchase, I'm offering a free report that's exclusive to my book and blog readers.

In *77 Good Habits to Live a Better Life*, you'll discover a variety of routines that can help you in many different areas of your life. You will learn how to make lasting changes to your work, success, learning, health and sleep habits.

Go Here to Grab 77 Good Habits to Live a Better Life:

www.developgoodhabits.com/free

In the *Ultimate Checklist Guide for Home Organizing*, you'll get a series of home checklists to help you stay on top of maintenance, cleaning, shopping, emergencies, energy savings, and more. This guide is the perfect companion for 10 Minute Declutter to support you with your new habit of streamlining and simplifying your home.

Go Here to Grab the 10 Ultimate Home Decluttering Checklists: http://bit.ly/1HGjpv5

Table of Contents

I

INTRODUCTION

The 10-Minute Declutter Challenge

"The more you have, the more you are occupied. The less you have, the more free you are."—Mother Teresa

Look around at the spaces in your home. Over the years, you've accumulated a houseful of possessions. Some items are useful and necessary. Some might even bring you pleasure, comfort and fond memories.

Probably, though, most of your stuff is simply clutter—items that are disorganized, misplaced or simply no longer needed.

Yet you still hang on to them.

Perhaps you're at the point where all this "stuff" is driving you crazy and that's why you've picked up this book.

The good news?

When you organize and eliminate clutter, you free yourself from stress and anxiety by eliminating feelings of overwhelm.

Decluttering gives you renewed energy, inner peace and more "mental space" to enjoy the meaningful, joyful aspects of your life.

Clutter is often a reflection of our inner selves. If we feel disorganized, out of sorts, depressed, stressed out or insecure, it shows up in the way we manage our daily lives.

Organizing your clutter is a path to healing emotional blocks and inner confusion. As you reclaim control over your stuff, you'll feel better about yourself and have more positive energy. You'll also feel more confident and in control of your life.

Researchers at UCLA's Center on the Everyday Lives of Families studied 32 middle-class families and how they live at home with their stuff. They chronicled their findings in Life at Home in the Twenty-First Century: 32 Families Open Their Doors, a book that revealed how addicted to material things we are as a society and how much stress clutter creates.

Anthony P. Graesch, an assistant professor of anthropology at Connecticut College and co-author of the book, made the following statement: "We've never had as much stuff in a single family's home as we do now. In part it is related to this most intense consumer society in which we live."

Accumulation has become a way of life for most of us.

You don't have to be a "hoarder," a shopaholic or a disorganized person to suffer from excess clutter.

Our culture reinforces accumulation, spending on luxury items and focusing too much time on material things instead of experiences and relationships. We've been taught the false narrative that more stuff equals greater happiness.

At some point, however, we find ourselves drowning in papers, clothing, toys, books and other objects. We realize all this stuff isn't creating more joy and peace of mind. Instead, it's extracting joy from our lives and becoming a proverbial albatross around our necks.

If you are at this point with your clutter, take heart. This book is designed to help you gain control of your life by controlling your clutter.

We understand how busy and demanding life is, and how difficult it is to tackle a huge project like organizing an entire house. Simply making a decision about where to store something or whether or not to throw it away can feel daunting and frustrating.

Fortunately, we have a simplified process that makes decluttering so easy and painless, you'll actually come to enjoy it.

This book outlines **a decluttering program that's broken down into 10-minute, bite-sized increments that are quick,**

painless and easy to fit into your hectic schedule. Day by day, you'll chip away at this project without feeling that sense of overwhelm that often pops up when you are faced with a daunting task.

Within a few weeks, your rooms will be completely organized, clean and arranged to perfection. Also, your most important (and meaningful) items will be displayed or stored exactly as you wish. Not only will your space become more organized and streamlined, but also you'll feel happier, lighter and less stressed out.

We explain exactly how to achieve these results in *10-Minute Declutter: The Stress-Free Habits for Simplifying Your Home.*

Who Are We?

Barrie is the founder of an award-winning personal development site, Live Bold and Bloom. She is a certified personal coach and online course creator, helping people apply practical, evidence based solutions and strategies to push past comfort zones and create happier, richer, more successful lives. She is also the author of a series of self-improvement books on positive habits, life passion, confidence building, mindfulness and simplicity.

As an entrepreneur, a mom of three and a homeowner, Barrie knows firsthand how valuable and life-changing it is to simplify, prioritize and organize your life and work in order to live your best life.

Steve (or "S.J.") runs the blog Develop Good Habits, and he's the author of a series of habit-related titles, all of which are available on Amazon at HabitBooks.com. The goal of his content is to show how continuous habit development can lead to a better life.

Instead of lecturing you, he provides simple strategies you can start using right away. His goal is to show how you can make lasting changes by developing one quality habit at a time.

The "Barrie and Steve" Declutter Challenge...

This book is a collaborative effort between Steve and Barrie. We both provide information and knowledge from research, outside experts and our personal experiences.

In fact, we decided to do our own decluttering challenge to give you real-world insight into the decluttering process, to make sure the 10-minute tasks we suggest are doable in 10 minutes, and to ensure the resources and insights we provide will actually work for you.

While we were writing this book, Barrie was preparing her house for sale, which was perfect timing for the decluttering challenge. In order to sell the house (and prepare to downsize to a much smaller home), she needed to go through every drawer, every closet and every nook and cranny to decide what to keep, what to toss and what to store for the future. Every day, right after lunch, Barrie would tackle a 10-minute project, working her way through the rooms of a home measuring more than 3,800 square feet.

Having lived in the same house for nearly twenty years, this project was about as massive as it gets. She experienced all of the challenges of decision making, reorganizing and releasing material things. In the end, she found the process liberating and enlightening. Creating more space, living with less and properly organizing what remains creates a sense of freedom and peace that's hard to explain until you go through the process.

On the other hand, like many people, Steve struggled with keeping his "stuff" in check. While he understands the importance of a clear space, he often found it hard to get rid of items that once seemed important.

Things changed in late 2014 when Steve decided to take massive action and eliminate the possessions he didn't need. Each morning, he'd wake up, complete his *Habit Stacking* routine and then immediately declutter for 10 minutes. Once he finished his decluttering session, he would begin his workday.

What did Steve discover? The "10-minute declutter habit" had a snowball effect on his life. At first, it was difficult to stick to this schedule. However, after a week of following the same routine, he instinctively started to organize and eliminate items even when he had already completed his 10-minute decluttering session for the day. Simply put, decluttering became an automatic action instead of a daily task he had to cross off his to-do list.

As you can see, both authors had different experiences when they decided to minimize their lifestyles. Over time, Barrie has become more organized with her possessions, while Steve is just starting to embrace the idea of reducing clutter. By reading about their experiences, you will discover effective strategies to use with your own decluttering efforts.

Three Important Reminders...

There are three things you should keep in mind as you read this book.

First, you'll notice that we use the third-person tense (e.g., "Steve remembers..." or "Barrie suggests...") when sharing anecdotes about our experiences. This was done specifically to make it easier for you to follow the narrative of the book. We admit it's a bit clunky, but you'll find it's easier to grasp the information if you know who is telling the story.

Next, you'll need a few items to help you thoroughly declutter your home. Each section of the book includes examples of items that can help you get organized and eliminate clutter. We've also compiled a shopping list for you and published it on Steve's blog.

Finally, this challenge is designed for someone who lives a hectic life, so we suggest doing everything in 10-minute blocks of time. That said, if you feel inspired, feel free to continue decluttering on those days when you have extra time. The important thing is to commit to this habit for *at least* 10 minutes a day.

Who Is This Book For?

"10-Minute Declutter" is for anyone who is tired of being surrounded by items they don't need and wants to regain control of their living environment.

This book will be a good fit if you:

- feel overwhelmed by the sheer volume of your material possessions
- can't easily get in closets, move around rooms, or find things quickly
- feel indecisive and confused about what to do with all of your stuff
- have little time to tackle big organizing projects
- feel embarrassed and drained by your clutter
- find yourself attached to things you know you don't really need
- get complaints from your spouse or family members about your clutter
- simply desire a more organized, minimalist lifestyle

If you're married or have a partner who lives with you, you might want to share this book with them. Perhaps you can work together to knock out these 10-minute decluttering projects.

If you have children, you can assign them short decluttering tasks that are easy and fun. This will teach them the importance of personal responsibility and how to live in a tidy space.

The bottom line?

If you have a desire to live in an organized, simplified home, you've come to the right place. Throughout *10-Minute Declutter*, not only will you learn the skills you need to organize your home, you'll also discover an actionable strategy to implement immediately.

We have a lot of ground to cover, so let's jump in and discuss how your *mindset* might hold you back from eliminating meaningless items in your life.

8 "Reasons Why" You Haven't Decluttered

Odds are, you've watched (or least heard about) the television show *Hoarders*. If you haven't, here's a brief synopsis. Camera crews go into a home that is <u>filled</u> with junk. A mental-health professional and a professional organizer interview the occupant, ask why the person can't get rid of all the clutter that has piled up, and try to help them make decisions about whether to keep, donate or throw away items.

Honestly, Steve feels this show often exploits the people they're trying to "help" for the sake of entertaining viewers, but there's a valuable lesson to be learned by listening to the language used by many hoarders. They often have what they feel are legitimate reasons for not getting rid of certain items.

Now, we're not suggesting you're a hoarder, but we do feel it's important to pay close attention to the **excuses** you have for why you haven't decluttered your space. We suggest you go over each one and ask yourself if you've *ever* felt the following.

#1. You feel guilty.

Grandma knitted you an ugly sweater *five years ago*, and you've <u>never</u> worn it. Uncle Bill bought you a nifty beer-making kit that's still sitting in your basement, unopened. You won a nice set of steak knives as second prize for your office's sales contest.

We've all had experiences like this.

Family and friends are nice enough to get us some heartfelt gifts that we....well, just don't use. The problem? Getting rid of these gifts seems heartless and mean-spirited.

But let's speak plainly here—it's time to get over the guilt.

Guilt should *never* play a part in your decision to keep an item. The decision should be based on the actual importance of an item.

As an example, you would never throw away the 200-year-old family bible because it has a significant value to you and your children. On the other hand, you shouldn't be afraid to throw away the pink bunny suit your aunt made for you.

#2. You have a sentimental attachment.

People also hold on to items that remind them of important events or experiences. A ratty old concert T-shirt, an ugly tchotchke from Rome and three boxes of old comic books are all examples of items that have sentimental value. All *seem* important because they're reminders of happy times, but you're probably keeping them only because you have a sentimental attachment to them.

Obviously, you want to hold on to items that are really important to you. It's only a problem if you have a sentimental attachment to each and every item in your home.

The solution is to allow a limited amount of space for sentimental items, such as a single display shelf or limited wall space to display your favorite collectibles. If you want to keep something, there needs to be a designated spot for it. This makes it easier to evaluate the importance of every possession.

As an example, Steve used to keep every T-shirt he received after running a race. After completing a few hundred races over the last few decades, he has more shirts than one person could possibly wear.

Now, whenever he goes to a race, he examines the shirt, and if it doesn't look or feel right, he'll simply give it back. He also limits the number of shirts he wears during training runs.

Whenever he gets a new shirt, he looks at his existing collection and gets rid of one he no longer wears. By using these simple tactics, he's no longer buried under a pile of running shirts he rarely uses.

#3. You "might" need it someday.

We often keep items out of fear of needing them at some point in the future. Everything you own *could be* used someday, but the truth is, someday rarely comes.

The solution is to assign a date or event to every item. If you do not currently use the item, or at least have a date or event when you will use it, then it needs to go. (We'll go over how to do this in a later section.)

#4. You spent money on it.

It's easy to keep an item because you spent money on it. You never use it, but getting rid of it is admitting that you made a mistake with the purchase.

In business, there is a term called the *sunk cost fallacy* where you make poor decisions *after* a bad investment. The money is gone and there's no way to recover it, so you try to find a way to "validate" the purchase.

For instance, let's say you bought a book at an airport kiosk. On the plane, you read the first 20 pages and realize it's not what you wanted. The store is back at the airport you just left, so there's no way to return the book. Because you've already spent money on it, you force yourself to keep reading it.

Paying for an item should have little bearing on your decision to keep it. The only question should be how much an item is worth to you today. If you no longer need it, then it should go.

#5. You consider it an investment.

Some toys and household items acquire a "cult status" after many years and accrue value with time. We often view those items as possible investments that can make us money in the future.

The truth is, you can never predict what will be valuable down the road. For every Honus Wagner rookie card, there are boxes of Marvel's New Universe comic books that have little value.

"Possible" future value shouldn't mean a thing.

Is the item worth something right now?

If it is, then sell it.

If it's not, then give it away.

The equation is simple enough.

#6. You want to boost your image.

Going back to the *Hoarders* example, many people keep possessions to improve their mood and outlook on life. Some have marginal lives, so their items represent lost self-esteem.

It would be bad advice to tell you to "get over it." The fact of the matter is, if your self-esteem is tied up in objects, you need to work on yourself as much as you need to work on eliminating items from your life. A psychologist or other professional may be able to help you work through your issues.

#7. You are saving items for family members.

This is an area where there *is* a solid reason to hold on to certain possessions. You don't want to throw away your children's things simply to succeed at building the 10-minute declutter habit.

That said, there is a limit to how much you should save. Steve's rule of thumb (and what his parents saved for him) is to save only as many items as you can fit in one large box. Once you fill the box, you have to make hard decisions about what you're keeping for family members who *don't live* in your home. An even better solution is to give them their boxes and let them make the hard decisions.

#8. You find comfort in your possessions.

In a weird sort of way, "ownership" provides a sense of security and comfort. When you buy an item, there is a feeling that you've improved an important area of your life.

To quote the narrator from *Fight Club* (one of Steve's favorite movies):

"You buy furniture. You tell yourself, this is the last sofa I will ever need in my life. Buy the sofa, then for a couple years you're satisfied that no matter what goes wrong, at least you've got your sofa issue handled."

Many people are obsessed with the idea that everything has to be perfect or immediately accessible, so it's easy to fall in the trap of trying to buy possessions that will cover every possible situation that might arise.

There is a small bit of truth to all eight excuses. What's unfortunate is how often people allow these limiting beliefs to prevent them from getting rid of their items.

That's why it's important to be unemotional about the decluttering habit. The more wiggle room you leave in the process, the more useless junk you'll keep in your home.

Err on the side of getting rid of anything you don't really need. For instance, Barrie has thrown or given away hundreds of items in the past 20 years, yet she can count on one hand the number of times she honestly said, "I wish I'd kept that" after getting rid of something.

14 Benefits of the Decluttering Habit

S till not convinced the decluttering habit is right for you? In this section, we cover fourteen reasons why it'll have a positive impact on every area of your life:

#1. It's safer and healthier.

Having a few misplaced items on your desk isn't a safety issue. However, when the number of items you have starts to get into hoarder territory, then your possessions become a legitimate danger to you and your family.

Extreme clutter can cause all sorts of health and safety issues. It can become a nest for bugs and vermin, a fire hazard and a breeding ground for airborne viruses. Clutter is like a magnet for household dust, which is a combination of dirt, skin cells, pet dander and chemicals. Dust contains bacteria, fungi and dust mite particles that can trigger allergies.

The more stuff you have, the harder it is to keep your home clean and dust-free. Even if you clean your house regularly, you may still have boxes of stored items, stacks of books or bins of toys that rarely get the attention they need.

#2. It saves you money.

Organizing can save you money.
Here are three reasons why:

a. You can sell things you no longer use. (We'll cover this in the next section.)
b. You won't mistakenly purchase an item that you already own—one that's probably buried in a drawer somewhere in your home.
c. With a clean and organized space, you'll minimize the desire to buy most stuff because you don't want the additional clutter.

There's something powerful about eliminating unwanted items from your life. You start to closely examine every purchase, which ultimately saves you from wasting money on things you don't really need.

#3. It helps the environment.

We're going to avoid a long discussion about how our consumerist society is hurting the planet, but it *is* important to do little things that decrease your carbon footprint. When you have an organized home, you consume less, and when you consume less, you create less trash. When you create less trash, you're making smart decisions for the environment.

#4. It gives you more time.

If you have fewer material things, you don't have to spend as much time caring for and maintaining them. You'll also spend less time organizing and storing possessions, and more time doing things you really enjoy. The initial declutter habit will take some time, but it will help you save time once you pare down your possessions. In a way, it's like making a financial investment. You put the time in now to enjoy the dividends in the future.

#5. It decreases stress.

A chaotic and cluttered area is a major source of stress. Most of us subconsciously (or consciously) want to live in an organized environment. When an area is cluttered, some part of your mind feels agitated because each item represents a task you have yet to complete.

Additionally, an organized area can have a calming effect. Imagine serene Buddhist monks. Do you see them meditating in a messy area, or are they in a beautifully manicured and minimalist setting? Hopefully, you know the answer to that question.

As the Dalai Lama reminds us, "Simplicity is extremely important for happiness. Having few desires, feeling satisfied with what you have, is very vital: satisfaction with just enough food, clothing, and shelter to protect yourself from the elements."

#6. It increases energy.

The Chinese concept of feng shui states that open areas have more "flow" to them.

This flow gives you energy, abundance and happiness in the home. With increased energy (and less time dedicated to dealing with unimportant clutter), you'll experience an increased capacity to tackle the things that truly matter.

#7. It improves focus.

Think about how it feels to try to finish a work project when you have papers strewn across your desk, or how hard it is to concentrate on preparing a meal when your kitchen is a mess. Extraneous stuff absorbs your focus and pulls your attention away from the task at hand. With fewer distractions, you'll be able to focus on important tasks.

#8. It makes you productive.

The ability to find any item, plus the mental benefits of living in an organized environment means you'll get more done throughout the day. When you no longer feel overwhelmed and stressed by your possessions, you'll have more energy to devote to work and life tasks that improve your quality of life.

#9. It increases confidence.

When you look at a clean area every day, you feel a sense of pride, even a sense of control, from mastering your personal space. This feeling of accomplishment fosters a dramatic increase in your confidence.

#10. It increases appreciation.

"Stuff" will never make you happy, but when you keep only the "stuff" you really need, you develop an increased appreciation for certain items and their impact on your life. You also focus more on the non-material pleasures of life and your gratitude for people, experiences and nature. You discover what's really important.

#11. It helps your love life.

If you're single (and actively dating), taking someone home to a clean environment is much sexier than bring them to disorganized chaos. If your living space is a reflection of who you are, then you're sending the message that you've got your act together.

If you're in a relationship, your significant other will appreciate living with a tidy person instead of someone who is constantly creating clutter.

#12. It improves socialization.

When your home is a mess, you might avoid asking people to come in. Knowing that your home is always clean and neat allows you to easily invite friends and coworkers to visit without worrying about what they'll think.

#13. It makes you disciplined.

Discipline is like a muscle.

The more you use it, the stronger it gets.

It takes some effort to keep an area decluttered. Doing this every day strengthens your ability to take action—even when you don't feel like it.

Just think about how the military trains soldiers. Commanding officers usually start by teaching new recruits to keep their areas nice and tidy. They enforce strict rules because discipline can be life saving when it's time to make difficult decisions as a soldier.

#14. It provides a fresh start.

Let's face it…we often get bogged down by the day-to-day grind. Life is often boring and predictable. It can feel like we are spinning our wheels and getting nowhere. There's no better time than right now to make a significant change.

Decluttering is a great change. We consider this a keystone habit because it affects so many other aspects of your life and personality. If you are looking for a fresh start and want to make big changes in your life, then decluttering is the way to go.

The Decluttering Mindset

L ike most people, you might be someone who enjoys the thrill of purchasing a new item.

Perhaps you enjoy seeing beautiful things in your home, or maybe you like keeping up with the latest fashions. No matter the reason, we often view our material possessions as symbols of our success, status and level of income.

However, you've probably also noticed how short-lived these feelings of pleasure are. You long for the new gadget or trendy outfit, but once you have it, your attention moves on to the next thing you want. The desire for "stuff" is a beast that constantly needs to be fed.

The problem?

Eventually your home ends up filled with items that have little value to you. They no longer serve a purpose and often end up in the bottom of a junk drawer.

Our question to you:

If you no longer "want" certain items, why are you holding on to them?

According to minimalist blogger and author Andrew Hyde (who owns just fifteen items), "Americans in particular like to be prepared for the worst-case scenario, having separate cookie cutters for Christmas and Halloween. We seldom consider how negligible the consequences are when we run out of something or are unprepared. Nor do we consider how high the consequences are for being over-prepared…"

In other words, we often hold on to our possessions out of fear and a need for security.

Unfortunately, this security is an illusion.

Having more things doesn't mean you'll survive tough financial times. Actually, spending money on pointless junk often means an increase in debt or not having enough money for the truly important things in life.

According to Cornell psychology professor Thomas Gilovich, who has spent years researching consumption and happiness, **experiential purchases** bring people far more happiness and life satisfaction than material purchases. It's *how* we spend our time that makes us happy, not what we own.

As you begin developing your decluttering habit, we'd like you to consider reorienting your life away from materialism and more toward experiences.

As you give away items, let them go willingly with the knowledge that they may benefit someone else. Consider streamlining all of your possessions to the most essential, useful and meaningful.

Only you can decide what those items are, and it may take several decluttering sessions to get comfortable with reducing the number of possessions you own.

However, you can decide right now to minimize your spending on material things going forward and to make any future purchases mindfully.

As you experience the freedom of letting go and living with less, you'll be less inclined to bring more clutter into your home. This new mindset will save you money, time and energy. It will also allow you to spend those resources on what truly matters most to you.

Okay, before we move on to the "how-to" portion of this book, we want to go into detail about how the decluttering habit can actually have a positive impact on your bottom line as well as your quality of life. Specifically, we provide a simple plan for making money by off-loading your stuff. As the saying goes, "One man's trash is another man's treasure." It you're not using it, release it graciously to someone else—and make some money at   the   same   time.

How to "Cash In" with Your Clutter

Think back to our discussion of the sunk cost fallacy. Odds are, one of the reasons you hold on to certain items is because you spent money on them. Fortunately, there are a few ways to recoup some of your losses while minimizing clutter at the same time.

In this section, we'll go over how to make money with decluttering by selling off your unwanted items. But before we get to that, there are two things you should keep in mind.

First, "I am going to sell that" is a common excuse people give for *not* decluttering. So it's very important that you only worry about reselling items that have actual, real-world value. Don't just put something aside and say, "I will sell that." Put things aside with specific plans on where, how and when you'll sell them.

Second, selling your possessions takes time. The point of this book is to give you simple 10-minute routines for decluttering. Selling a heap of your stuff will take longer than that.

Consider selling your items one at a time for your "10-minute habit." That includes the time you need to take pictures, upload them to a website, assign a price and write a product description.

You could also use the time to set aside items for a bulk trip to a physical store or organize items for a future garage sale.

Trying to sell every item in your home is very time consuming, and it's often not worth the time or effort. Think of it this way: if you spend ten minutes preparing an item and your net return is one dollar, that means your time is worth six dollars per hour. At that rate, you can probably find a better use for your time.

However, depending on what you plan to sell and the value of the items, your efforts could prove to be very lucrative. If you aren't sure how valuable your item is, take a look at Craigslist or eBay to see the going rates. A few minutes of research could save you a lot of time and energy during the process.

How to Get Started with Reselling

The first step is to take a hard look at your possessions.

Do clothes have any (even small) stains, tears or obvious sign of wear? Do your DVDs and CDs have any scratches? Are your books full of pen marks, or do they show excessive wear or discoloration?

If certain items look very used, then it's best to go with option #1 listed below.

Option #1: Thrift Store Charities

Donating items is not exactly "selling" your stuff, but places like the Red Cross, and Goodwill accept all sorts of donations, plus they'll give you a receipt for tax purposes.

Dropping off your items at these places is the simplest way to get rid of things that have inherent value but are hard to resell.

Now, if you donate to charities that are *not* the ones listed above, research each charity to find out if it's a *registered non-profit organization.* If you live in the United States, a simple tool for figuring this out is Melissa Data.

Finally, if you're donating strictly for tax purposes, be sure to get an itemized list from an employee. That way, if you ever get audited, you'll have a specific breakdown of everything you gave away.

Option #2: Consignment Shops

A consignment shop is a step up from the thrift store. Shop owners are very discriminating about the items they accept, and they won't accept any merchandise that doesn't have a good chance of being resold. In other words, not only should your clothes be clean and in good condition, they also have to be "in style."

Consignment shops work in two ways. They either buy items from you directly, or they sell items for you and give you a percentage of each sale—typically 40 to 60 percent of the price.

To find consignment shops near you, simply do a local search on Google, get their phone numbers and ask the owners what items they accept and how much they offer.

Option #3: Freecycle

Technically, this is not "selling," but an easy way to get rid of valuable items is to post them on Freecycle. Once you post an item, an email goes out to people signed up in your area.

All you have to do is drag the items to the front of your home, and people will come and get them. The first person to arrive is the one to get your freebies.

The benefit of this option is you don't have to get in your car and drive somewhere. In fact, you don't even have the hassle of dealing with people. Your items just magically disappear.

With Freecycle, you save time, which is like saving money for some people. If you run a business (like both authors) and know that your time has a specific dollar value, then avoiding the hassle of a drive will ultimately save you cash.

Now, there are a few drawbacks to this option. The first, obviously, is you don't get any cash for your items. Second, Freecycle is only available in certain areas, so this option might not work for you. However, there might be a similar program in your area. A quick Google search will tell you.

Option #4: Eaglesaver

Eaglesaver is a fairly hassle-free way to get rid of old textbooks, books, DVDs, CDs and video games. The items must be in good condition. That means no excessive scratching, tears, broken cases or water damage.

You won't get a lot of money per item, but the process is really simple:

1. Get instant quotes for items from the website.
2. Complete the order by printing a free shipping label.
3. Ship the items.
4. Get paid by check or PayPal.

If you're someone who is embracing digital media (like downloading files instead of purchasing CDs and DVDs, or purchasing Kindle books instead of print books), then Eaglesaver is a simple way to eliminate the entertainment items you no longer need.

Option #5: Craigslist

Craigslist is probably the most famous way to get rid of your possessions while recouping some of your money. The process is also relatively straightforward:

1. Sign up.
2. Take nice picture of your items.
3. Upload the pictures.
4. List the item.
5. Assign a reasonable price (remember to price it to sell, not to make maximum profit).
6. Wait for emails to come in.

As a future "10-minute declutterer," you might find Craigslist to be a great option because it's the buyer's responsibility to come get the item. All you have to do is create the ad and answer a few questions.

Craigslist is a particularly good place to sell furniture because moving these items can be more of a hassle than the extra few bucks you would get from selling them elsewhere.

One last thing…

Selling on Craigslist means a stranger will show up at your home. While 99.99 percent of buyers are perfectly normal, there is a small chance that you could be inviting someone dangerous to your home. Use caution and schedule the transaction for a time when someone else will be with you.

Option #6: eBay

EBay is similar to Craigslist, but you don't have to deal with random strangers showing up at your door. The challenge of using this site is that there are many more steps involved with the selling process, so you should only consider it if you have a lot of items to resell.

Our advice is to use eBay to resell items that are in demand, such as comic books, collectible toys, antiques and dolls. Just think of items that people want and would be willing to bid against one another to get.

The important thing to remember with eBay is *you* have to ship the item. This makes smaller items the most cost effective to resell. Large, heavy items will eat up your margins unless you charge the customer a high shipping price.

Reselling small collectibles can add up to a nice amount of money. While it's true that one man's junk is another man's treasure, avoid the temptation to use eBay for eliminating everything in your home. As we've discussed before, this strategy can become a form of procrastination on your 10-minute declutter habit.

Option #7: Amazon

Okay, maybe we're biased. Barrie and Steve generate income from Amazon by selling books, so we both love this option, but Amazon is also a great option for reselling some of your possessions.

Like eBay, Amazon is best used for "collectibles" and other in-demand products. It's unlikely you'll be able to sell your used electronics or old clothes.

Now, there are two ways you can sell on Amazon.

First, you can sell and ship items yourself as a Professional Seller, which costs $39.99 per month. You can find out more about this program here: http://amzn.to/1Amb9Rh

The second option is to join the Fulfillment by Amazon (FBA) program. This means you ship the item to Amazon, they store it and when it sells, the folks at Amazon ship it to the customer. This means they take a bigger cut of the profits, but it gets unwanted items out of your hands and out of your house, which is the main point of this book.

You can find out more about this program on the FBA homepage: http://amzn.to/1BiQaK1.

Option #8: Swap Meets, Garage Sales or Car Boot Sales

These sales are another way to get rid of random items, but it's not a tactic we recommend because your per-hour cost is often not worth the effort to set everything up. In our opinion, a far better option is to spend your time decluttering and focus on reselling your "big ticket" items via Craigslist, eBay or Amazon.

That said, one option is to look for church, town-wide or neighborhood-wide sales. Some communities put these together and do a great job with advertising them. The end result is you get a massive influx of people ready to buy your possessions.

#9: Gumtree (or other local classified ad websites)

Since Barrie and Steve live in the United States, they have never used Gumtree. But if you live in the United Kingdom, it's a better option than Craigslist.

Besides Gumtree, there are a lot of country-specific classified sites. Simply go to Google, type in the keyword phrase "classified ads" and add your country. What you'll get back is a list of resources for reselling your possessions.

All right, we've come to the end of the introduction portion of this book. You know now *why* decluttering is important, how certain excuses are holding you back and a few strategies for reselling your items. So let's move on and talk about the plan you'll follow to build the decluttering habit.

II

HOW TO FORM THE DECLUTTERING HABIT

8 Steps to Form the Declutter Habit

Both Barrie and Steve talk a lot about habits in their books. If you want to make sure the declutter habit "sticks," then you need to follow a specific blueprint for building new habits.

In this section, we review the same eight-step plan Steve recommends to his readers for building *any* type of habit.

Step #1: Focus on the Decluttering Habit

There is a concept called ego depletion, which is "a person's diminished capacity to regulate their thoughts, feelings and actions."

Ego depletion impacts our ability to form new habits because our supply of willpower is spread out among all the areas of our lives. Because of this, it's important to work on only one habit at a time. That way, your store of willpower can be channeled into building that one habit, increasing the odds of success.

For the sake of this book, we ask that you completely focus on the 10-minute declutter habit and avoid adding anything "new" to your schedule.

Step #2: Commit to Decluttering for 30 Days

Some people say it takes 21 days to build a habit, while others claim it takes up to 66 days. The truth is that the length of time really varies from person to person and habit to habit. You'll find that some habits are easy to build, while others require more effort. Our advice is to commit to decluttering for the next 30 days (or a month to keep it simple).

Step #3: Anchor Decluttering to an Established Habit

Your decluttering efforts should **not** be based upon motivation, fads or temporary desire. Instead, decluttering should be instilled in your life to the point it becomes automatic behavior.

The simplest way to do this is to incorporate the teachings of B.J. Fogg and his "Tiny Habits" concept. What you want to do is to commit to a very small habit change and take baby steps as you build on it. An important aspect of his teaching is to "anchor" the new habit to something you *already* do on a daily basis.

"After I wake up, I will walk into the targeted room for the day and begin my 10-minute decluttering session."

"After I put my kids to bed in the evening, I will spend 10 minutes decluttering."

You get the idea. Simply find a habit you already do consistently, and then anchor your new behavior to it.

Step #4: Pick a Time for Decluttering

The best time to declutter is the time that works best for you. If you work away from home during the day, you'll need to knock out your 10-minute declutter habit either before or after work. That said, remember that decluttering habit needs to happen immediately after your trigger so you'll be reminded to follow through on a daily basis.

Sticking to this trigger is especially important, as you want to create momentum and enjoy the feeling of immediate success. Starting and stopping your clutter-busting commitment will leave you feeling frustrated, which interferes with your brain's ability to turn it into an automatic action.

Be sure your trigger is something that happens every day (if you want to work on decluttering seven days a week). If you want to skip weekends or declutter every other day, you can certainly do that, but it will take longer for the habit to form. If possible, work on decluttering every day for the first four to six weeks.

If you decide to work on your clutter before you leave for work, the trigger should be something like brushing your teeth, taking your shower or making coffee.

Waking up early is, in itself, a difficult habit to establish. If you have to wake up earlier to add the decluttering habit to your new routine, consider picking a different time to declutter. If you don't have trouble waking up early, then the mornings might be a perfect time. Just be sure you set yourself up for success with this new habit by avoiding any pitfalls that might throw you off track.

If you work on your decluttering once you come home from work, choose a time (and trigger) when you are still energized and won't have many interruptions. This might be immediately after you walk in the door or right after dinner. If you're a night owl and get your second wind after 9:00, then you can declutter before going to bed.

Barrie works from home and uses eating lunch as a trigger for performing her clutter-busting habit. Because she's already interrupted work to eat, it's easy to move into a quick 10-minute decluttering project.

Step #5: Take Baby Steps

As discussed in *Tiny Habits*, the best way to create a new routine is to make micro-commitments and focus on small wins. Motivation alone won't help. The danger of relying on motivation alone is that you don't have a back-up plan for when you're not in the mood to declutter. Instead, you need to turn the habit into an automatic behavior.

So while your long-term goal is to declutter for 10 minutes at a time, you should start slow and focus on building the routine first. It's more important to stay consistent and not miss a day than it is to do the whole 10 minutes.

Examples include:

- Organizing one dresser drawer
- Bringing a collection of Goodwill items to your car
- Clearing off a single shelf in your closet

Yes, these activities seem overly simplistic. That's the idea here! You want to commit to something so easy that it's *impossible* to miss a day. Then, when you've built the habit, you can do the full decluttering routine for 10 minutes.

Step #6: Plan for Your Obstacles

Every new routine will have obstacles. When you know in advance what your obstacles are, you can take preventive action to overcome them.

Examples of common obstacles:

- Boredom with the routine
- Uncertainty of what to sell
- Uncertainty of what to donate
- Feelings of anxiety or guilt
- Not knowing where to start

If you anticipate these obstacles, you won't be blindsided by them.

The simplest solution is to use a concept called "If-Then Planning" where you create scripts to help you overcome these obstacles. Here are some examples:

- "If I'm having trouble completing a morning declutter routine, I will commit to a new time and trigger."
- "If I find myself making multiple trips to the store, I will take time to go through my entire home, write one large shopping list and use it during my next trip to the store."
- "If I'm struggling to eliminate items in one section of my home, I will delay this project and move into a different room."

See how each of these statements helps you overcome the specific challenges that you face? Our advice is to create similar statements for all the roadblocks that might arise with your daily declutter habit.

Step #7: Create Accountability for Decluttering

Track your decluttering efforts and make public declarations about your new routine. According to the Hawthorne effect, you're more likely to follow through with a commitment when you're being observed by others. To stick with the decluttering habit, you should let others know about your commitment to this habit.

Post updates on social media accounts, use apps like Chains and Coach.me to track your progress, work with an accountability partner or post regular updates to an online community related to the habit. Do whatever it takes to get reinforcement from others in support of your new routine.

Never underestimate the power of social approval. Simply *knowing* you will be held accountable for your habit keeps you focused and consistent.

Step #8: Reward Important Milestones

Decluttering doesn't have to be boring. Focus on building a reward system into the process so you can take time to celebrate the successful completion of your goals. The reward you pick is up to you, but it's important to celebrate those big moments along the way.

Keep in mind that a reward doesn't have to break the bank. You could check out a new movie, enjoy a night out with your significant other or simply do something you love that doesn't cost a lot of money.

We tend to underestimate the importance of having "fun" while building habits. Often, though, having a clear reward for regularly completing an action will help you to stick to the new routine.

Those are the eight steps for forming the decluttering habit. Simply follow the steps outlined and determine the best time to perform your habit, and you'll quickly add this routine to your day.

Now that you understand the basics of habit formation, let's talk about how to get started.

Your Basic Decluttering Shopping List

Before getting started, you'll need to purchase and gather supplies for your decluttering efforts. At first, this project will create a big mess, which could create a stressful environment. The solution is to get certain supplies ahead of time to make it easier to organize the items you're eliminating.

Now, the purchasing phase is one aspect of our program that will take longer than 10 minutes. You'll take a trip to the store or spend time on a retail website—like Amazon— to do your shopping. It's important to complete this step in advance because it'll save you lots of time and frustration down the road.

Below is a list of general supplies you'll need for most of the projects outlined in this book. As a reminder, we've also created a special page that profiles some of our favorite items: http://www.developgoodhabits.com/decluttering-supply-list/

There are also specific suggestions for supplies within each "mini-project" in this book. We suggest you make additional supply trips once you have a better feel for how and where you want to store your stuff.

Here's what we recommend to get started:

- Timer (to set for 10 minutes)
- Six to ten cardboard boxes in several sizes (to stage items to keep, donate or move to another room)
- Markers and pens

- Notebook
- Post-it notes
- Stick-on labels
- Sturdy trash bags
- Shelf liner
- Rubber gloves
- Step stool or small ladder
- Basic household cleaning supplies
- Paper towels or cleaning rags

Once you've purchased these items, you can get started. Our suggestion is to start with the room where you spend the most time. Let's talk about that now.

How to Pick Your First Decluttering Project

One struggle people have with decluttering is not knowing where to begin. We suggest you start with the rooms where you spend most of your time. Tackling these rooms first will give you an immediate boost of emotional energy, motivate you to keep going and quickly improve your peace of mind.

Most people spend the majority of their time in the bedroom, kitchen and family room. If you're like Barrie and Steve (who work from home), your office might be another area to consider.

Another recommendation is to complete an entire room before beginning another. Consider each room to be a mini project that creates a sense of accomplishment once you complete it. This will make it easier to stick to the habit instead of trying to do everything piecemeal in various rooms throughout the house.

That said, if it works better for you to complete 10-minute projects randomly, or if you'd like to group certain spaces to declutter sequentially (e.g., all closets, all drawers, all bookshelves, etc.), then you can do that as well.

There are no hard and fast rules related to the order of this process. Really, the important thing is to stay committed to decluttering and do this 10-minute project every day.

Deciding *What* to Keep...

As we mentioned earlier, there are a myriad of reasons why we hang on to things or neglect to organize them. One of the most common reasons we get stuck when decluttering is we can't decide what to do with our things.

You might pick up an object and think to yourself, *"I might use this one day. Someone in the house can use it. It's too nice to throw away. Should I give it to Goodwill? Didn't Aunt Sue give this to me? It might hurt her feelings. Oh forget it."*

Then you put it right back where it was because you feel too much guilt about getting rid of it. The decision seems way too complicated.

We often attach meaning to objects, especially if they were gifts from a loved one. It feels like we're showing disrespect to people (and memories) if we throw away or give away these unwanted possessions. We feel anxiety and guilt about letting them go, even though we know they are cluttering our lives.

Sometimes the guilty feelings arise from other voices (real and imaginary) that still affect our ability to make decisions around our stuff.

As an example, a reader of the blog "Unclutterer" submitted this question to the editor of the site.

"While helping my sister unclutter for her move, I came across some dolls in dresses she'd worn as a baby and a huge (unfortunately not her style) afghan a great aunt had crocheted.

We both agreed that if it were just up to us, we probably wouldn't keep these items...but instead of our own voices in our heads saying, 'You can't get rid of that!' it was our mother's voice. How do you unclutter when it's not really sentiment, but more guilt, that stands in the way?"

Guilt serves its purpose when we've actually done something wrong, but it shouldn't be a deciding factor when it comes to our stuff.

As adults, we have the right to let things go if they are no longer useful or important to us. There may be certain sentimental items you want to keep, but the choice should be a positive one, not one that comes from a place of guilt.

There are ways to create reminders of these items that have personal meaning without actually keeping the items. You could:

- Take photographs of them and store them on your computer.
- Create a sentimental scrapbook with the photos.
- Gift certain items to family members who would appreciate them, knowing they are staying in the family.
- Put them in a "holding pen." Place the items in a sealed box for a year. If you haven't opened the box by the following year, throw it away without looking inside.

Remember, you're not enjoying these sentimental items if they're stored away or never used. Not only do they create clutter, but also they create negative energy and emotions. Once you get in the habit of eliminating them, we promise you won't continue to feel anxiety or regret.

Now, to help you make decisions about decluttering, we've created fifteen parameters to help you move forward. Let's talk about those parameters.

15 Questions to Ask While Decluttering

You have to ask yourself certain questions as you go through your possessions. Ultimately, these questions will help you decide whether something should stay or go. Remember, you only have 10 minutes to complete each decluttering task, so to get maximum results, you'll need to learn how to make quick decisions.

Here are fifteen types of questions you should ask:

1. *Is this item useful? Can it save me time, energy or money? Does it fulfill a need or purpose? If not, let it go.*
2. *Do I like it? If not, let it go.*
3. *Does it make my life easier in some way? If not, let it go.*
4. *Have I worn it, used it, found pleasure in it or looked at it in the **last year**? If not, let it go.*
5. *Does it energize me or drain me? If it drains you, let it go.*
6. *Is it broken beyond repair or damaged in some way? If so, let it go.*
7. *Is the information it provides outdated (e.g., old books, magazines, videos, etc.)? If so, let it go.*
8. *Am I holding on to it out of guilt? If so, let it go.*
9. *Have I finished using it and see no reason to use it again? If so, let it go.*
10. *Does it reflect the person I am today or a past version of me? If it reflects the past, let it go.*
11. *Do I already own something similar? If so, let it go.*

12. *Will I complete this (e.g., a knitting project, an unfinished book)? If not, let it go.*
13. *Am I spending too much time weighing the pros and cons? If so, let it go.*
14. *If I had to downsize to a much smaller house, would this go with me? If not, let it go.*
15. *Does this have any historical or potential financial value (e.g., an item passed down for several generations)? If not, let it go.*

Not all of these questions will apply to each item. If you get stuck on a particular item, use the questions as part of your decision-making process. Odds are, your uncertainty means your mind is searching for an *excuse* for keeping the item.

If you can't make a decision, use one of your boxes as a "Maybe" staging box and toss the item in there. You can revisit these items at a later date or seal the box up and put a date on it with the word "Maybe" written on the outside. Keep the box for a year; if you never open it, toss it.

Now that you have a framework for making quick decisions, it's time to create the staging area for your decluttering project.

How to Stage Your Declutter Habit

You can get a surprising amount of decluttering done in 10 minutes. Barrie has cleaned out drawers, organized a linen closet and cleaned out underneath a sink—each within that 10-minute limit.

However, 10 minutes doesn't give you enough time to store items you want to save, take other items to Goodwill or run down the street to give a box of toys to your neighbor.

A solution is to stage these items in boxes and place them in a temporary area until you're ready to do something with them. There are seven things to consider when working with a staging area.

#1. If you're working in one room over the course of several days (or weeks), and you have an out-of-the-way section to keep your boxes, then this is the best solution.

On the other hand, if the room is small or cluttered, the last thing you want is more clutter. You'll need to assign a room or table somewhere in the house to keep your boxes until they're moved out of the home.

#2. Be sure to label each box if you have items to give to friends and family, donate, sell online or sell at a garage sale.

#3. Rather than making several trips to Goodwill, you might want to stage your donation boxes until you've finished the entire decluttering project.

#4. If space is an issue and you don't know where to place certain items, store them in your basement, garage or other storage rooms until you complete your decluttering project and know <u>exactly</u> where everything will go.

#5. If you want to sell items online or at a garage sale, you'll need to store them until they're ready to be sold.

#6. If you want to write off donations for tax purposes, having the items in a central location makes it easier to itemize them before they're removed from the house.

#7. If your staging room starts to overwhelm you, then by all means, make some trips to the donation center or call for pickup. The point is to save time and energy, but you might need to clear out your staging room before you completely finish decluttering.

Barrie has used her formal dining room (the least-used room in the house) as a staging room, but has encountered the issue of guests coming over or holiday events occurring in the middle of decluttering. Think about these possible disruptions and have a plan B for a staging location.

Now that you understand how to effectively choose and use a staging area, let's go over the final preparations you'll make before starting your first decluttering project.

How to Prepare for Your First Decluttering Project

One of the biggest problems people face with decluttering is they start too big and end up with a bigger mess than the one they had before starting. When you clean out a closet, you often end up with piles of clothes, shoes and boxes strewn all over the closet and bedroom.

Our goal is to help you declutter in <u>manageable bites</u> so you don't leave a trail of clutter in your wake. The best way to do that is through preparation.

Before you dive into your first decluttering project, let's take a minute to review all of the steps to take to start on the right foot and minimize any stress and mess.

You want to have all of these items covered before your start date.

1. Pick your start date (give yourself a week for preparation).
2. Review the principles of habit creation by selecting a time, anchor and reward for your decluttering routine.
3. Purchase and gather the basic supplies you'll need.
4. Determine the room where you'll begin and create a list of the rooms you'll tackle next, in order of priority.
5. Print out or write down the "15 Decluttering Questions" to have handy as you begin making decisions.

6. Choose a staging area for boxes of items you're storing, selling or giving away.
7. Get four large boxes and designate one box for each of the following: "Store," "Sell," "Donate" and "Give Away." Do the same with four smaller boxes. You can use the small boxes for small items in drawers, on your desk, etc. Then you can place the small boxes inside the bigger boxes with the same designation.
8. Put your big boxes in your staging area and have your other supplies and cleaning materials in the project space the night before you start.
9. Tell your family what you're doing and enlist their support. The last thing you want is someone undermining your efforts and re-cluttering your organized spaces.
10. Make it fun! Choose some great music to listen to while decluttering. Have plenty of water handy, and make sure your timer and reward are in the room with you.

It's Time to Get Started!

You're all prepared and ready to dive in to your first decluttering project.

The first 10-minute project for each room (or space) is to assess the following:

- What size boxes are needed for this area?
- What section should be first?
- What additional supplies are needed?
- How much cleaning is involved?
- Is heavy lifting required? (If so, then you might need assistance.)

Use your notebook to make notes about any additional supplies you'll need.

Don't buy the supplies yet—wait until you finish decluttering a few spaces and coordinate a supply run with another out-of-the-house errand.

One Last Thing…

There will be several areas in your home that you'll break down into multiple 10-minute projects.

For example, you won't clear out your entire basement in 10 minutes. Instead, it's better to chunk down this area and focus on smaller projects (like removing unused exercise equipment, organizing shelves or going through individual boxes).

There might also be times when you finish up one project and want to keep going and tackle another. That's fine, but try to stick with a series of 10-minute jobs rather than just diving in to a big undertaking. If you get tired or distracted, you don't want to be halfway through and left with a big mess.

These 10-minute chunks will help you manage your space, time and energy.

Okay, you now understand how the decluttering habit works, you have all the necessary supplies, your staging area is ready and you're armed with the right questions to ask as you're decluttering.

So what's first?

Well, as we said previously, the best strategy is to begin with your priorities—the rooms where you spend the most time. Unfortunately, not everyone who reads this book has the same priorities, so we'll start with the most obvious choices.

III

DECLUTTERING YOUR KITCHEN

Introduction

For many folks, the kitchen is the catchall room for every item that enters the house. Mail and keys wind up on the counters, school books are scattered on the kitchen table, coats and sweaters are slung on the backs of chairs and the bowl of pet food always gets kicked over as you're rushing around preparing a meal.

In many ways, the kitchen is more like the family room than any other room in the house.

Wouldn't it feel amazing to have not only a sparkling-clean kitchen, but also one that's streamlined, tidy and organized?

We feel that the kitchen is the best place to begin a decluttering project because it sets the stage for how you want the rest of your house to appear.

Now, some organizing experts will suggest you begin by clearing your counters first, which works well if you plan to tackle your kitchen in one decluttering event. But for this project, when you're working in 10-minute increments, you'll need to create space in cabinets, closets or drawers for those items you no longer want on the counter.

For instance, Barrie has found beginning with the lower cabinets often frees up space for some of those countertop appliances.

Here's a suggested plan for tackling your kitchen:

- Begin with the lower cabinets, moving left to right around the room.

- Move to the upper cabinets, following the same pattern.
- Move to the kitchen drawers, starting with the drawers used most often.
- Now with more space above and below, clear the countertops.
- Clean out and organize the refrigerator.
- Tackle the pantry starting from the top shelf and moving down.

> **Note:** If you keep items on top of your cabinets, clean and organize this space first, as it likely has collected a lot of dust that will fall onto your counters and floor. You don't want to have to clean twice.

Planning Your Kitchen Decluttering Project

Grab your notebook and pen and set your timer for 10 minutes. Survey your kitchen to assess the space (i.e., the amount of clutter and the supplies you'll need). We'll provide a few suggestions in the Tips area (at the end of this section). The important thing is to have your labeled boxes and cleaning materials available when you get started.

If you don't finish this planning before the timer goes off, put your notebook away and pick it up again tomorrow.

> **Note:** After you finish sorting and cleaning all the spaces in your kitchen, you can go back again to determine what organizers and storage containers are needed. After you purchase these items (and once everything is completely sorted), you can move items around and place them in the appropriate containers and organizers. Unless something needs to be installed, you can knock out several of these reorganizing projects in 10 minutes.

Section 1: Lower Cabinets

Set your timer for six minutes. Choose your first cabinet. If the cabinet has more than one shelf, begin at the top. Divide the shelf in half and take out everything on the left side of the shelf. Moving quickly, pick up each item and make a decision to keep it, toss it, give it away or donate it.

Be brutal in your decisions to let things go. If you haven't used it in forever, it's broken, you have too many or you just don't like it—let it go or put it in the storage box. If you want to keep it in the cabinet, set it aside for now. Put everything else in the appropriate boxes.

When the six-minute timer goes off, stop reviewing items (or hopefully you've finished) and use the remaining four minutes to clean that half of the cabinet and put your decluttering supplies away. If you haven't finished sorting, put the remaining items back in the cabinet and return to it tomorrow.

After you finish one shelf in a cabinet, move to the lower shelves in the same cabinet, working top to bottom, left to right, in 10-minute increments, leaving a few minutes for cleanup. As you work through the cabinets, make notes in your notebook about any organizers or containers you might want to purchase.

Lower Cabinet Tips:

- If you don't have paper, vinyl or rubber cabinet liners, create a separate 10-minute project to measure and cut the liners for your cabinets. You can place the cut liners in the cabinets easily after you clean each shelf.

- Be sure you leave some space in the lower cabinets for the countertop items you want to store. Appliances that are used infrequently should be stored out of sight.
- Barrie finds she ends up with an excessive number of plastic containers from take-out and prepared-food items. The lids get lost and the cabinet becomes a jumble of containers. Consider purchasing a stackable set of food storage containers and getting rid of the plastic mess.
- Store pots and pans in the lower cabinets closest to the stove—or consider a pot rack you can hang from the ceiling or on the wall. Consider purchasing pull-out organizers you can install in a cabinet for organizing pots, pans and lids. A magazine rack installed on a cabinet door is a great way to organize lids.
- Cutting boards and cookie sheets can be stored in an organizing rack with separators rather than stacking them.

Section 2: Upper Cabinets

The upper cabinets often hold breakable items like glassware and dishes. Since there are more individual items to remove, the process of removing them and cleaning the spaces might take a bit longer. Also, you might need to stand on a step stool or ladder, which slows things down. However, the decision-making process won't be difficult since you're dealing with a smaller quantity of items.

Follow the same steps you followed for the lower cabinets. However, you can't just toss breakables in your boxes to store or give away. There are two options that can help you stick with the 10-minute plan:

First, before removing items from the cabinet, take five minutes to review them and pull out anything you don't want to keep in the kitchen. Use the next five minutes to wrap the items in packing paper or bubble wrap and put them in the appropriate box. Then you can move on to cleaning and replacing items on the shelves the next day.

The other option is to follow the exact same process you followed for the lower cabinets, but set aside the items you want to box (on a table or countertop) until the next day. Then you use the next 10 minutes to wrap and box them.

Move through the upper cabinets, left to right and top to bottom until you have everything sorted, cleaned and put away or boxed.

Upper Cabinet Tips:

- You don't need to keep holiday dishes, Grandma's china or plastic plates in the cabinets you use most often. Only keep the items used on a daily basis in these priority sections. Keep fragile items in higher cabinets, in a china cabinet or in a storage area—far away from the kitchen.

- Put larger serving pieces higher up on shelves, or use them as display pieces in open or glass-fronted shelves.

- Place your everyday dishes and/or glassware in a cabinet over the dishwasher for convenience when you unload.

- Consider hanging stemware on a stemware rack under the counter. Barrie has found delicate crystal can get bumped and chipped on these racks, so use them for sturdier everyday stemware.

- Chipped and cracked glassware and plates are unsightly, unhealthy and dangerous. Chips and cracks can harbor bacteria, and they are more likely to break with heating and cooling. It's time to toss them.

- Consider purchasing space-saving organizing products to hang cups and stack plates.

- Most of us have an assortment of novelty mugs we've collected over the years. Unless you use them regularly, they are just taking up space. If you can't toss them, repurpose these items. You can create gifts by filling them with an assortment of teas or candies and wrapping them in colored cellophane. Here are some additional ideas for repurposing old mugs: http://bit.ly/1LwZdNw.

Section 3: Spice and Condiment Cabinet

Most of us have a cabinet for spice jars, cooking oils, vinegar, seasonings and dry baking supplies. You probably won't give away these items, but you might want to toss some of them.

Get started with a box that will hold the items while you sort and clean, and be sure to keep your cleaning supplies within easy reach.

Begin with the top shelf, moving left to right and then moving to lower shelves. Set your timer for three minutes, then pull out everything on the top shelf. Put the items in your box. Next, set the timer for two minutes and clean the shelf thoroughly. Put down a piece of shelf liner if necessary.

Set your timer again for five minutes and use the time to decide whether to keep or toss the items. Replace the items you're keeping on the shelf and make notes about any organizers or containers you'll want to purchase. Continue working through this cabinet in 10-minute increments over the next few days.

You'll need to check expiration dates on these items. If you aren't sure if something is too old to keep, it's generally better to toss it. Here are a few guidelines for the freshness dates on certain items:

- **Spices:** Whole spices will stay fresh for about four years, ground spices for about three to four years and dried leafy herbs for one to three years.
- **Oils:** Once opened, vegetable, canola, coconut, corn, safflower and sunflower oils last for one year; peanut and spray-can oils last for two years; olive oil lasts for two to three years; and other specialty oils are good for six months or less.
- **Vinegar:** Most types of vinegar have an indefinite shelf life; however, a very old bottle may begin to have a cloudy appearance or a dusty-looking sediment in the bottom of the bottle.
- **Flour:** Most flours last from four to six months on a shelf. You can extend that by keeping flour in the freezer.
- **Salt, Sugar, Pepper**: Sugar and salt lasts indefinitely; ground pepper lasts for two to three years.

(If you want to find more dry food expiration dates, check out the Eat By Date website.)

Spice and Condiment Tips:

Barrie keeps her most frequently used spices in a drawer by her stove so she can find them easily. She has a tiered rack in the drawer and arranges the spices in alphabetical order. Spices she uses less often are on a two-tiered turntable in the cabinet closest to the stove.

- Save cabinet space by getting a magnetic spice rack that mounts on the wall above or next to your stove.
- Purchase smaller bottles of spices you use infrequently, or buy your spices loose and put them in your own small jars to avoid waste.
- Consider storing dry baking goods in airtight containers in the freezer instead of keeping them in your cabinets. They'll keep longer and free up more cabinet space for other items.

- Get decorative oil and vinegar cruets that take up less space in your cabinet. Store larger refill bottles in the pantry to use when the cruets are empty.

Section 4: Under the Sink

The cabinet under the sink is often the most ignored space in the kitchen. It stays cluttered with cleaning supplies, pet products and an assortment of items you're afraid to store elsewhere. With plumbing pipes and a disposal in the way, it's also a hard space to keep organized.

Cleaning this cabinet may take longer than other cabinets, so this is how you'll spend most of your 10 minutes when you first begin…

Have your cleaning supplies handy (they may be stored in this cabinet) and a box to hold everything while you clean. Set your timer for 10 minutes; then pull everything out of the cabinet and place it in the box.

Thoroughly clean the cabinet and any bins attached to the cabinet doors. Add or replace shelf liner or a waterproof under-the-sink mat if necessary. If the timer goes off before you finish cleaning, place the cleaning supplies back in the cabinet and set the box of other items aside until tomorrow.

Once you have finished cleaning the cabinet, move on to sorting and organizing. Set the timer for 10 minutes and sort through the items in the box, placing any you want to keep back in the cabinet. Toss anything that is old or no longer useable. (Before you throw away cleaning products, read this article on cleaning product disposal.)

If you have time, consolidate duplicates of products into one container. Set aside useable products that you never use to give away. Items you use infrequently can be put in a box to store elsewhere and placed in the staging area. Make notes about any storage containers or organizers you might want to purchase. (These tasks may need to be separate 10-minute projects.)

Under the Sink Tips:

Sponges (and dishcloths) contain more germs than almost anything else in your house. Barrie uses paper towels to clean countertops and dishes because she feels it's more sanitary. However, it is more economical and better for the environment to use a sponge. If you use a sponge, it should be replaced every few weeks and sanitized nightly. Sanitize the sponge by rinsing it out and putting it in the microwave for one minute or putting it in the dishwasher when you run a load of dishes.

- If you use sponges or dish cloths, buy a few months' worth at a time so you are reminded to replace them frequently. Keep them stored in a wire basket or bin under the sink.

- Scrub brushes are slightly more sanitary than sponges or dishcloths and can be thrown on the top shelf of the dishwasher for sanitizing. Replace your brush if it's discolored, has a sour smell or has warped bristles.

- Purchase several small plastic or metal bins to group cleaning items together by category (e.g., floor cleaners, disinfectants or detergents). You can also use a large under-the-sink shelf designed to accommodate pipes and a disposal.

- Purchase stick-on hooks or a metal hook rack to install on the side of the cabinet or on the cabinet door for hanging brushes, rags and rubber gloves.

- If you don't have cabinet-door racks, purchase one for each door to store frequently used items such as tissues, dishwashing liquid, hand soap, lotion and the product you use to clean your counters.

Section 5: The Junk Cabinet/Drawer

Most of us have a few cabinets in the kitchen for storing miscellaneous items that don't fit anywhere else. This can include stacks of menus, loose change, over-the-counter medications, cookbooks and plastic novelty cups.

Most of us also have a catchall drawer that serves the same function, filled with things like small tools, scissors, tape, keys, scratch cover, lighters, small candles, coins and an assortment of other items.

These drawers are often convenient, but they are also natural accumulators of items that should be eliminated.

Barrie has one cabinet to the left of the kitchen sink where she keeps medications, adhesive bandages, lotions and thermometers on one shelf. On the shelf above that, she keeps boxes of teas, along with honey and other sweeteners, as she drinks tea regularly and this cabinet is easily accessible. In another "junk" cabinet, she keeps plastic cups, candles, water, coffee to-go containers and storage jars.

Regardless of how disorganized and mismatched the items in your junk cabinet might be, you can create a semblance of order.

Once again, start by moving top to bottom and left to right, unless this is just a single cabinet. Grab your cleaning supplies and notepad and set your timer for six minutes. Pull everything out of the top cabinet and begin sorting what you want to throw away, give away and replace.

When the timer goes off, use the remaining time to clean the shelf, put down or replace shelf paper and replace any items you want to keep. Continue moving through this cabinet over the next day or two, for as long as it takes to complete the sorting and cleaning in 10-minute increments. Make notes about any organizers you might want to purchase.

The junk drawer may take a bit longer to declutter because it tends to collect an array of small items, and it takes time to sort through them. Grab a few plastic grocery bags to use for sorting. Set your timer for four minutes and begin by emptying all of the contents of the drawer into a box.

Thoroughly clean the drawer and put down drawer liner. Set the timer again for six minutes and begin sorting similar items together in the plastic bags. Throw away any items you can't identify, items that are broken and items you no longer use and can't be used by others. Set aside items that need to be stored in other parts of the house. When the timer goes off, if you haven't finished, put the plastic bags inside the box and set them aside for the next day.

Junk Cabinet and Drawer Tips:

- Throw out any medications that have expired. For medicines that don't have expiration dates, unless you know you purchased them within the past year, it's best to toss them out. For the safest ways to dispose of medicines, check this site: http://bit.ly/1IZHrmu

- Store remaining medications in an airtight plastic container on the top shelf, out of reach of small children.

- Sort similar items together and put them in small plastic bins or baskets that fit on the shelves. Put frequently used items on the lower shelf.

- Use clear glass jars for small, loose items like change, bottle stoppers, matchbooks and other miscellaneous items you need but seem to get lost in the back of the cabinet.

- Use a napkin holder or file sorter to hold notepads, menus and other loose papers, or place them in an over-the-door pocket organizer.

Drawer Tips:

- Consider getting a cabinet-door organizer for plastic wraps and foil to reclaim valuable drawer space.
- Use space-saving drawer organizers for flatware, utensils, knives and spices.
- Consider putting frequently used utensils in a decorative container on the counter near the stove to save drawer space. You can even put flatware in decorative containers.
- A magnetic knife holder that attaches to the wall is a convenient and safe solution for your knives, freeing up even more drawer space. A knife block is also a great place to store these items.
- Be sure to measure the depth of your drawers before purchasing organizers or containers so your drawers close properly.
- Rearrange drawers based on convenience. Flatware should be near the plates and close to the dishwasher. Place cooking utensils near the stove, knives near the sink and oven mitts near the oven.

Section 6: Drawers

Your kitchen drawers are likely the most-used spaces in your kitchen. These drawers usually contain flatware, utensils, storage wraps and foil, knives, spices and other miscellaneous items. You might have a few deeper drawers that hold bread, pots and pans, and cookware. Having these drawers sorted and organized will save you time and keep your kitchen running like a well-oiled machine.

Your first 10-minute project will be an assessment of what you have in the drawers and how you might want to reorganize things to make moving around your kitchen easier. So grab your timer, your notebook and a pad of sticky notes. Set the timer for 10 minutes and, moving left to right around your kitchen, open each drawer and write down on a sticky note what's inside the drawer. Put the sticky note on the front of each drawer so you'll know at quick glance what's inside.

If you don't run out of time, make notes about how you might want to move things around to different drawers and create a list of any organizers or supplies you might need. If you don't finish this assessment in your first 10-minute session, then pick it up again the next day.

Your next 10-minute project will be to measure and cut drawer liner for each of your drawers. This may take two sessions depending on the number of drawers you have. Set these cut liners aside to have handy when you clean out each drawer.

Now you are ready to sort and clean each drawer, which you should be able to do within the 10-minute timeframe. Choose your most frequently used drawer to tackle first. This will probably be your flatware drawer. Set your timer for five minutes and have your cleaning supplies and boxes handy.

Remove everything from the drawer and thoroughly clean the empty drawer. Put down drawer liner if necessary. Set the timer again for five minutes and begin sorting through the items you pulled out. Begin by replacing the flatware you know you want to keep. Throw away anything that's broken. If you have mismatched pieces of flatware or other items that don't belong in this drawer, put them in the appropriate boxes to give away or store elsewhere. If you realize an item belongs in another drawer, go ahead and place it in that drawer.

You may realize you need better drawer organizers as you go along. Take a few pictures of the open drawer with your phone and measure the drawers' dimensions to use for a later shopping trip. Make notes in your notepad.

Move through the drawers in your kitchen, going from the most-used to the least-used drawers. For each drawer, set your timer for 10 minutes and follow the same process. If you don't finish before the timer goes off, set the items from the drawer in a box and resume your work the following day.

If you have duplicates of utensils or any other items, put those in your giveaway box. Throw away outdated dried herbs and spices from your spice drawer. Anything you haven't used in years, place those in your giveaway box. Put any dirty or dusty utensils, cookware or flatware in the dishwasher.

Drawer Tips:

- Consider getting a cabinet-door organizer for plastic wraps and foil to reclaim valuable drawer space.
- Use space-saving drawer organizers for flatware, utensils, knives and spices.

- Consider putting frequently used utensils in a decorative container on the counter near the stove to save drawer space. You can even put flatware in decorative containers.
- A magnetic knife holder that attaches to the wall is a convenient and safe solution for your knives, freeing up even more drawer space. A knife block can also be a great place for your kitchen knives.
- Be sure to measure the depth of your drawers before purchasing organizers or containers so the drawers close properly.

Section 7: Countertops

By the time you've started to declutter your countertops, you've done a lot of work! So, congratulations on sticking to the 10-minute decluttering habit and getting your kitchen organized. You're getting close to the end of this big project.

Having clutter-free, clean countertops is a great feeling. It's a boost of energy to see your kitchen free from extraneous papers, appliances and all the extras that often land on the counter. In fact, you might want to declare your kitchen counters a "clutter-free zone" where no one is allowed to park keys, schoolbooks, loose change or mail. This should become a sacred space where you only keep a few specific items.

It's best to declutter your countertops after putting away food, utensils and dirty dishes. If you need to clean up after a meal, that should be your first 10-minute project. Once the kitchen is basically clean, grab your notebook and boxes and set your timer for 10 minutes.

Take a look at your countertops and identify the appliances you don't use every day. Odds are, you don't need a food processor, mixer or bread maker sitting on the counter. You also don't really need to keep a cutting board or knife block on the countertop.

You should have created space in the kitchen cabinets in a previous project. Use this space to store any appliances you don't use on a daily basis.

Barrie keeps her food processor, juicer, smoothie maker, blender and mixer in cabinets below the counter. She uses her toaster, coffee bean grinder and coffee maker every day, so they are kept on the counter, but as part of her own decluttering project, she's decided to store them in a cabinet as well.

If your kitchen is small, then consider placing everyday appliances in a handy cabinet just to create a less cluttered look on your counters. If you don't have room under your cabinets for any of the appliances, set them in a staging area and consider moving them to your pantry, laundry room or a nearby closet.

Once you remove the appliances, begin moving left to right around your kitchen countertops. Pick up an item on the countertop and ask yourself, *"Does this belong here? Do I need it to be here?"* If not, put it in the appropriate box to either store elsewhere or give away.

Set a goal of having as little as possible on your counters. It's okay to have a plant or a few decorative items, but otherwise try to remove as much clutter as possible.

Once everything is removed from the counters and you're happy with the appearance, use another 10-minute session to thoroughly clean the counters, sink and stovetop.

Now your kitchen is sparkling clean, organized and streamlined.

Doesn't it feel great?

Countertop Tips:

- Barrie finds that countertops attract all of the sets of keys when people enter the house. Find a place to store keys so they don't clutter the countertop. Consider putting a key bowl in a cabinet, or take a look at these cool ideas for hanging your keys so they are handy but out of the way.

- Do you keep cookbooks on the counter? Consider taking photos on your phone of your favorite recipes so you'll have them handy but out of sight. If you love your cookbooks, store them in a basket under the counter or on a nearby bookshelf. Then pull out the one you need and replace it when you're finished.

- Do bills and other mail wind up on your counter? The best strategy is to sort mail as soon as it comes in the house, throwing away junk mail and filing away the rest. You can use an over-the-door pocket organizer (over your pantry or kitchen door) to sort bills and other mail until you're ready to deal with it. Or put all of the important mail in an out-of-sight basket until it's time to go through it.

- If you keep a drying rack on your counter for hand-washed dishes, consider putting the drying rack in the sink instead, or allow dishes to dry in the dishwasher. If you don't have a dishwasher, dry with a towel right away rather than letting dishes sit on the counter. It will save you time in the long run.

- If family members drop their schoolbooks, briefcases, backpacks, purses or wallets on the kitchen counter, it's time for a reeducation program. Announce that the kitchen is a "clutter-free zone," and offer alternatives for storing their stuff. Get them involved in creative ideas for storing their personal items.

- Make a habit of clearing your countertops every night before bed so you can wake up to a clean, uncluttered kitchen.

Section 8: Refrigerator

If you've ever cleaned out and scrubbed your refrigerator, you've learned the hard way how long it can take. Not only is the refrigerator crammed with food, jars, cartons and bottles, but it's also the palette for spills, drips and crusty junk that has the strength of a diamond. For many people, cleaning a refrigerator can be a daunting proposition.

Most people tackle the refrigerator as one big project, but you don't have to commit several hours of your day to get this space clean. We've broken it down into easy 10-minute projects. In fact, you can tackle some of these while you're already in the kitchen preparing a meal, waiting for water to boil or waiting for the oven to preheat.

Grab your cleaning supplies (paper towels, glass cleaner, kitchen soap, a small scrub brush or old toothbrush, and a bowl of warm water) and set your timer for four minutes.

Begin on the top shelf of your refrigerator. Remove everything from the self and set it on the counter. Thoroughly clean the shelf and the walls of the refrigerator around that shelf, scrubbing crevices with the toothbrush. You can remove the shelf to clean it if necessary.

Set the timer again for three minutes and sort through the items you removed, checking expiration dates. Throw away anything that's expired or any leftovers over four days old. Place any expired items that are in recyclable containers near the sink and put everything else back on the shelf. Be sure to wipe off any jars or containers that have drips on them before replacing them.

Set the timer again for three minutes and wash out any recyclable containers and put them in your recycle bin. Barrie saves some of these containers to reuse for leftovers or food storage.

Repeat this 10-minute process for each individual shelf, drawer and bin in your fridge. Depending on how much is in your refrigerator, you might be able to tackle more than one area in 10 minutes.

After you've cleaned out every shelf, drawer and bin, take another 10 minutes to review your food items and decide on any storage products you might need. (See Tips below.) Make a note in your notebook of any purchases you want to make.

Follow this same process for each shelf and bin of your freezer. Remember to wear rubber gloves when working on the freezer to protect your hands. Since you're only working in 10-minute increments, you can leave the frozen items out on the counter while you clean a shelf. However, if you decide to keep going, place the items in a cooler while you work.

After you clean the inside of the fridge and freezer, use another 10 minutes to thoroughly clean the outside and top of the entire unit. Remove any old photos, school papers and drawings that have seen better days, and start fresh with a sleek, clutter-free refrigerator.

Refrigerator Tips

During your decluttering project, you might discover duplicate bottles of ketchup, soy sauce, olives and other items. You can combine some of these items, but be sure you check expiration dates before you do. You don't want to combine fresh items with expired ones.

- To maximize space, don't store unopened cans of soda and single-serve bottles in the fridge. Store unopened, non-perishable products in the pantry.

- Consider putting some refrigerated food in the freezer instead to save space. Milk, cheese, meats and many other foods can be easily and safely frozen.

- If you have take-out leftovers, take them out of the big restaurant containers that block your vision and put them in smaller containers. For your own home-cooked leftovers, it's better to separate large amounts into multiple small containers for easy reheating and to minimize bacteria.

- Store foods in clear, stackable containers so you can see the food easily.

- When you bring home meat, double-bag it and store it on a platter in the meat drawer or on the bottom shelf to avoid leaks that could contaminate other food.

- Before you put fruits and veggies in the fridge, pat them down with a paper towel to get rid of extra moisture. Read this article on the best way to store fruits and vegetables to maintain their taste and freshness.

- Consider keeping eggs in the original carton you purchased them in to prevent breakage.

- Remember, the "best before" dates apply to unopened foods. Once a container is opened, the food deteriorates much faster, even when stored in the refrigerator. Once you open a container, be sure to write the date on it so you know whether or not it's safe to eat.

Section 9: Pantry

Your pantry is a space that screams for attention. It often gets neglected because the door is kept closed and only opened when you need a certain item. As a result, there is little incentive to keep this area organized.

The trick to maintaining a decluttered pantry is to have a system where you can easily find things and to store items according to the "last in, last out" rule to prevent spoilage.

Like the other sections of your kitchen, get started by grabbing your notebook and cleaning supplies (including a step stool, dust broom, warm soapy water, and cleaning rags or paper towels). You probably won't need your sorting boxes, unless you want to donate items to a food bank.

Set your timer for four minutes and begin with the top shelf. Remove everything from the shelf. Sweep off the shelf and then clean it thoroughly with the warm soapy water.

Set the timer again for six minutes and review all of the items you pulled out. Throw away anything that has expired. Check any open containers of baking goods, rice, pasta and other grains for bugs or evidence of other pests. Throw away anything questionable. (See Tips below for ideas on storing these items.) If there are items you want to donate, set them aside to place in your donation box.

Follow this process for each shelf in your pantry, allotting 10 minutes for each shelf. If you can complete two or more shelves in 10 minutes, then go for it! But plan for 10 minutes per shelf to clean, sort and replace items.

Once you have cleaned and sorted the entire pantry, create another 10-minute project to assess organization. Barrie likes to organize the pantry by category, keeping like items together.

As an example, all canned goods go on one shelf; baking goods are stored together in a bin; pasta, rice and other grains are in a different bin; and snacks are grouped together on a separate shelf.

Keep the items you use most often within easy reach. You might want to put lighter items up higher, heavier items on the bottom shelf and small items on a lazy Susan in the middle.

Organize the items on your shelves to your liking. Make notes in your notebook about any storage and organization supplies you want to purchase. Once you have these supplies, you can go back and put the food items in the appropriate containers.

Pantry Tips:

- For storing canned goods, consider getting a tiered can rack that allows you to put newer items in the back and older items in the front. This ensures you always use older food first.

- Get an assortment of clear plastic storage containers and bins. Use the containers to store and properly seal food items like pasta, baking supplies, dried beans and snacks. Not only does this protect those items from pests, but also it makes your pantry look beautiful. You can group some of the smaller related containers in the larger bins (for example, put containers with flour, sugar and cornstarch into one big bin).

- If you need extra space in your pantry, a slide-out or roll-out cabinet organizer can really help give you more space.

- If you have a large pantry with plenty of room, use this space to store small appliances and bulk packages of water, paper goods or soft drinks.

- Use a permanent marker or label maker to label containers and bins for quick and easy reference.
- Keep bulk paper goods like paper towels, paper plates and cups, and plastic utensils in a bin on a higher shelf since you don't need them daily and they weigh less than heavier items.
- Consider getting a bin or holder for plastic grocery bags if you reuse them. You can even use an empty cardboard soda case or tissue box to store them.
- If you have small children, put your snacks in containers on a higher shelf. With snacks out of reach, it is easier to manage their snacking.
- Consider creating an inventory of your pantry items so you know what you have and when you need to purchase more.

IV

DECLUTTERING YOUR LAUNDRY ROOM

How to Declutter Your Laundry Room

Your laundry room should feel the way you want your clothes to look and feel—clean, crisp, neat and smelling fresh. Unfortunately, many laundry rooms morph into mudrooms and broom closets full of random items. In addition to laundry supplies, it's easy to store dirty shoes, backpacks, pet food and other junk. It's like the junk drawer for the entire house.

The question is:

Wouldn't it be nice to walk into a clean laundry room where everything is tidy and in its proper place?

Fortunately, it's pretty easy keep your laundry room decluttered once you have a system in place.

Let's start with the clothes you have in the laundry room right now. If you have a load in the dryer or in a laundry basket waiting to be folded, set your timer for 10 minutes and begin folding.

Once you've finished folding, take another 10 minutes to put away the clothes. Yes, that will take you out of the laundry room, but leaving your clothes sitting in the laundry basket is a bad habit that adds clutter to the room. So go ahead and knock that out.

Now that you've handled the existing laundry, it's time to deal with the room itself. Grab your notebook, sorting boxes and cleaning supplies and set your timer for 10 minutes.

If there is anything sitting on top of your washer and dryer, take it all off and thoroughly clean the outside of the washer and the crevices where dirt, soap residue and hair accumulate.

If there's any trash, wet lint or coins in the washer, clean those out as well. Then move on to the dryer, wiping off the top, the knobs and the inside, if necessary. Then clean out the lint filter.

Now that the washer and dryer are cleared and cleaned, your next 10-minute projects will involve moving around the room, left to right and top to bottom, sorting through items, putting them in the appropriate boxes and cleaning the space.

If you have open shelving or cabinets in your laundry room, start at the top, working on one small section at a time (as you did in the kitchen). Set your timer for 10 minutes, remove the items from the shelf, clean the shelf, add shelf liner if necessary and replace any items you want to keep. If you have time after cleaning and replacing everything, go through the remaining items and put them in the appropriate boxes to store elsewhere, give away or donate. Again, be sure to read this article on cleaning product disposal before you throw away any supplies: (http://bit.ly/SFZqZf).

Go through every shelf or cabinet in the laundry room, working top to bottom, until they're cleaned and organized. By now, you should have a feel for how much space you can do in 10 minutes, so divide up the laundry room accordingly.

After you finish the cabinets and shelves, set your timer for 10 minutes and look around the laundry room for items stuck in corners, behind the door or on top of the cabinets. Pull out any items that shouldn't be kept in this room and put them in the "store elsewhere" box. Throw away items that are broken and put everything else in the donate box.

Use another 10-minute session to determine what should be stored on shelves, in cabinets and on the floor. Make notes about any storage supplies or organizers you might need (see Tips below). And moving forward, be sure to keep your washer and dryer clear of clutter.

Laundry Room Tips:

- Rather than stacking mops and brooms in a jumble against the wall, get a broom and mop holder you can mount against the back of the laundry room door to keep these items out of sight.

- Use baskets, caddies or plastic bins to store similar items. Laundry detergent, bleach and fabric softener can go in one container. Cleaning supplies can go in another. Pet food and pet items can be stored in separate container. You might keep pet food in a closed can or bin next to the pet bowl.

- If your laundry room has limited space, consider buying an inexpensive shelving tower where you can store extra baskets and bins with additional items like cleaning rags, batteries, light bulbs and other necessities.

- Have a different colored laundry basket for every person in the house. On laundry day, separate clothes by the person and enlist their help in folding and putting away their own laundry. Even children can do this chore.

- If you have a cat and keep the litter box in the laundry room, consider getting a litter box system with a shield or cover that reduces litter spillage on the floor. The best way to reduce litter odor is by cleaning the box regularly. If you aren't good about that, you might consider an automatic self-cleaning box.

- If your laundry room does serve as a mudroom, consider a hanging rack for coats, purses and backpacks, with space for holding dirty shoes and boots.

- If you air-dry sweaters and other items that can't go in the dryer, consider a wall-mounted drying rack so you can lay items flat and allow the air to flow on both sides while still saving space in the room.

V

DECLUTTERING YOUR
MASTER BEDROOM

Introduction

Similar to the kitchen, the master bedroom is a multifaceted decluttering project that will require several days (even weeks) of 10-minute projects, but it's well worth the effort because it's one of the most important rooms in the house. Your master bedroom should be your sanctuary—a place that feels peaceful, calm and inviting.

In fact, results from a survey by the National Sleep Foundation (NSF) suggest that people actually sleep better when their bedrooms are comfortable and tidy. There's no question, creating the right environment in your bedroom will help your sleep, your sex life and your overall mental health.

Many of us ignore our bedrooms because we *only* sleep there. We hop out of bed, leaving the blankets in a tangle and the bed unmade. We throw clothes around the room, leave laundry in piles and let strange things accumulate under the bed.

Fortunately, you *can* reclaim this space as your private retreat, not only for better sleep, but also as a space for relaxation, privacy, romance and peace.

In this section, we'll cover the main bedroom, leaving the master closet and bathroom as separate projects.

Here's a suggested plan for tackling your bedroom:

- Be sure to make your bed in the morning. It sets the stage for a clean room and is considered a "keystone habit"— one that triggers you to perform other positive habits. It should only take you a minute or two. By the way, if you're someone who keeps several dozen decorative pillows on your bed, plus your stuffed animals from your youth, it's time to feng shui your bed. Check out these beautiful bedrooms on Pinterest to find your "pillow style."

- If you have stuff under your bed, that will be the next project. Sleeping on top of disorganized junk can't help your sleep, and it contributes to an accumulation of dust and bugs.
- You'll make several circles around the room, clearing basic clutter first.
- You'll make another circle dealing with surface areas (the tops of chests of drawers, bedside tables, etc.).
- After surfaces are organized and cleaned, you'll begin with drawers, moving top to bottom.
- If you think you'll need drawer liner for any drawers, create a separate 10-minute session to measure and cut the liner to have it ready when you need it.
- Once the room is completely decluttered and organized, you can go back and clean everything thoroughly.

So let's move on to the first 10-minute project, which is the pre-planning before you begin the actual work.

Planning Your Bedroom Decluttering Project

Grab your notebook and pen and set your timer for 10 minutes. Survey your bedroom to assess the space, the extent of the clutter and basic supplies needed as outlined previously. Make note of any organizing containers or storage essentials you think you might need (see recommended products in Tips below). Be sure to label all boxes and have cleaning materials available, as well as your laundry basket for any dirty clothes lying around.

If you don't finish this planning before the timer goes off, put your notebook away and pick it up again tomorrow.

Note: After you finish sorting and cleaning all of the spaces in your bedroom, you can go back again to determine exactly what organizers and storage containers you'll need. Once you purchase these items (and everything is completely sorted), you can move everything around and place them in the appropriate containers and organizers.

Section 1: Under the Bed

Set your timer for two minutes and make your bed neatly. (If your sheets are dirty, use the two minutes to strip the sheets and throw them in the washer.) Then set it again for three minutes and pull out everything that's under your bed.

Use the remaining time to sort through the items under the bed and put them in the appropriate boxes to store elsewhere, give away or donate. Throw away any trash or unusable items.

If you don't finish this sorting in 10 minutes, set the remaining items aside and complete the project the next day.

Under the Bed Tips

- Try to keep the space under your bed a clutter-free zone. Your bed should be an independent island of peace rather than a hiding place for stuff.
- If you are truly short of space for clothes or storage and need the space under your bed, use an under-the-bed storage container on casters with a lid to keep the items clean and tidy. Use plastic bins rather than canvas, wood or cardboard because they are the best defense against dust and bed bugs.
- Be sure you measure the distance from your bed frame to the floor to make sure your storage boxes will fit. If it's a tight space, don't get boxes on casters.

- If you don't want the boxes to be visible under the bed, consider getting a bed skirt that covers the space between the bed and the floor.

Section 2: Basic Bedroom Clutter

Set your timer for two minutes and make your bed. Then set it again for four minutes and grab your laundry basket. Moving left to right around your room, pick up any clothes (clean or dirty), dishes, books, papers and any other stuff that doesn't belong on the floor, the bed or any of the surfaces.

When the timer goes off, if you haven't finished picking up these items, use the remaining four minutes to continue around the room, putting items in your laundry basket. Set the basket aside for the next day.

If you do finish picking up, use the remaining four minutes to deliver the items to the appropriate rooms—put clean clothes in drawers or the closet; deliver dirty clothes to the laundry room; and put dirty cups and dishes in the dishwasher. You can finish putting things away in another session if necessary.

Basic Bedroom Clutter Tips:

- If you have stacks of clean clothes to put away, this may take one full 10-minute session. As you put the clothes away, go ahead and sort them to make sure you find pieces that you can donate. If you do, put them in the appropriate boxes.
- If you have important papers that need to be sorted, put them in a file or box and put them in the room that has a

desk in it. You'll sort the files when you declutter this room.

- If you save old magazines, now is the time to trash them. You can find most magazines online, and these stacks are just taking up space. If you "must" keep them, put them in a labeled box and then put them in your storage area.

- The same goes with printed books—those stacks by your bed are cluttering up your space. If you're reading this book on a Kindle, you already know how it saves space and is easier to hold. Steve had a really hard time giving up buying printed books, but now he reads 95 percent of his books on the Kindle. Save a few of your favorites and donate the rest.

Section 3: Bedroom Surfaces

Once you've organized the clutter lying around the bedroom, it's time to focus on your furniture. Grab your cleaning supplies, boxes and a few small baggies for those random items that wind up on top of your dressers and beside tables.

Set your timer for two minutes and make your bed. Then moving left from the door of the bedroom, start with the first piece of furniture that has a surface. (For Barrie it would be the chest of drawers.) Set the timer for three minutes and remove everything from the surface of the chest or table. Thoroughly dust and clean the piece of furniture. Replace a lamp or telephone if necessary.

Set the timer for five minutes and sort through the items you removed. Put small items like buttons, coins, etc. in a zippered plastic bag. (You can go through these later in another 10-minute session.) Try to keep the surface as clutter-free as possible. If you don't absolutely need an item or really want it on that surface, put it in the appropriate box. All those tchotchkes really do is gather dust.

Continue moving around the room to each piece of furniture with a surface—bedside tables, TV cabinet, bookcase and linen chest. Follow the same 10-minute process, beginning with making your bed and moving around the room until all of the surfaces are cleared, cleaned and sorted.

Bedroom Surface Tips:

- One or two nicely framed photos on a dresser looks nice, but a huge cluster often looks cluttered. Pick some favorites and consider hanging the rest in a stylish grouping on the wall.
- If you and your spouse tend to toss coins, keys, nail clippers and other pocket items on the chest of drawers, put a small decorative bowl either on top of the chest or in the top drawer to hold these items.
- A bedside table with drawers will keep the surface area clean. All of those items you need next to you at night (tissues, medications, TV remote, glasses) can be neatly stowed away rather than cluttering the table. If you don't have drawers in your bedside table, consider getting a decorative basket that sits under the table to hold these necessities.
- Consider putting a houseplant or two in your bedroom on one or more of these surfaces. They have a soothing effect, look beautiful and actually improve the air quality of the room.
- If you are a lover of printed books, find a small bookshelf to keep in your room or elsewhere in the house. You can find inexpensive bookshelves on Amazon (see suggested products) or at secondhand stores, IKEA or Target. Barrie has narrowed down her book collection to some of her favorites, and she uses bookshelves around the house for decor and accessorizing.
- In general, keep in mind that *less is more*. The cleaner the surface, the better you will feel in your room. Too much stuff creates distraction and low-level anxiety.

Section 4: Drawers

Now that your room is free from surface clutter, it's time to dive in to the drawers. Again, you can move left to right around your room to tackle any pieces of furniture with drawers or cabinets that need to be decluttered.

The biggest job is likely the drawers that are full of undergarments, pajamas, T-shirts, sweaters and random items—so let's start with those.

If you're married or living with your partner, you may have two separate chests or dressers, or you may share one. Be sure to talk with your partner before decluttering and organizing his or her stuff—or better yet, enlist their participation in the process. It's hard to thoroughly declutter your room if your partner isn't on board.

Grab your sorting boxes, cleaning supplies and notebook. Set your timer for two minutes and make your bed if you haven't already. Set the timer again for four minutes, make some quick notes about any organizers you might need for the drawers and dump out the contents of your top drawer on a clean surface. Wipe down the inside of the drawer and put down drawer liner if necessary. Set the timer again for four minutes and begin sorting through the items in the drawer as quickly as you can. Make four piles as you sort—one to throw away, one to store elsewhere, one to donate and one to keep.

Be sure to revisit the **fifteen purging questions** mentioned before to help you sort clothing items.

If something is old and tattered, permanently stained, missing its match, doesn't fit, or if you've never worn it, then it shouldn't find its way back in the drawer. You won't miss it once you let it go, so try to make quick decisions and move on. As you sort, place items in the appropriate boxes and replace anything you want to keep. See the tips below for ideas on storing specific items in your drawers.

Some drawers might require two or three 10-minute projects, like the sections for socks and underwear. If you don't finish a drawer before the timer goes off, place the remaining items in a bag or box and tackle them the next day.

Keep working through the drawers of your chest or dresser and then continue around the room with any other drawers or cabinets that need purging. Clean the interiors of drawers as you go, immediately after you remove everything.

Bedroom Drawer Tips:

- Once you finish decluttering and sorting and have more space, you can rearrange items in your drawers. Put similar items together (underwear with bras or T-shirts, socks and tights) in the same drawer if you have limited space. Consider grouping items by color or utility.
- Put delicate hosiery in plastic baggies to prevent pulls and runs from wood splinters in the drawer.
- Bras take up a lot of drawer space, so consider arranging them in your drawer nested together, cup to cup, the way they are arranged in drawers at lingerie stores. This also helps maintain the shape of the bra.
- If your drawers don't have built-in compartments, consider getting dividers or make your own with empty tissue boxes with the tops cut out. This helps keep small items from getting lost in your drawer. Another option is using the divider that comes with a box of wine for storing socks, underwear and other small items.

- Rather than stacking your T-shirts, you can create more room and make it easier to identify items by "filing" them. Fold your shirts as you would when stacking; then fold each one in half again and stand them up on an end like a file folder. As you pull out a shirt, you make less mess than you would with pulling one out from the middle of a stack. You can also roll your T-shirts to save space.

- If you're short on room in your drawers, only store the current season's clothing in the drawers and put off-season items in a storage bin in your closet or another storage area. Also consider hanging jeans and khakis rather than folding them in the drawer.

- If you have old T-shirts you really love for sentimental reasons but never wear, consider repurposing them. Barrie has a friend who made a quilt with the front pieces of all of her son's old T-shirts.

- Sweaters and knits should always be folded, not hung. Use a deep drawer for sweaters and place cedar blocks inside to keep moths away.

- Create one or two 10-minute projects to bag items to give away and to store anything you need to put in a different room or in storage.

Now that you've finished decluttering your entire bedroom, take another 10- minute session to give it a final cleaning. You've already dusted surfaces and cleaned out drawers, but you still might need to vacuum under the bed or around the room. Dust or vacuum curtains and wipe down windowsills, picture frames and the TV.

Take a good look around the room to make sure you like the arrangement of the furniture, or determine if you might want to remove a piece of furniture that makes the room look cluttered.

Once you have everything placed as you like it, take a photo of your beautiful room to help remind you to keep it this way—

and congratulate yourself for creating this decluttered and clean oasis that you can finally enjoy.

VI

DECLUTTERING YOUR BATHROOMS

Introduction

Since you just decluttered your master bedroom, try moving immediately to your master bathroom. With that said, the steps outlined in this section apply to *any* bathroom in your home. If your master bathroom is the biggest in the house, then once you've completed it, the rest should be a breeze.

You won't have too much work in the bathroom because it's small and there's limited space. But it's amazing how much you can cram under the sink and in a linen closet. Let's get started on making your bathroom more like a spa retreat than a football locker room.

Here's a suggested plan for decluttering and cleaning your bathroom:

- Because of the small area, try cleaning each section in a single 10-minute project.
- Begin by doing a sweep of basic clutter, clothes and dirty towels.
- Next, move on to the bathroom surfaces—countertops, around the tub and any shelves or furniture in the room.
- Organize the bottles, soaps and shampoos in the shower.
- Declutter and organize the linen closet.
- Clean any remaining areas like the toilet, the floor and any rugs in the room.

Planning Your Bathroom Decluttering Project

Grab your cleaning supplies, boxes (although you might not need them), some trash bags and your notebook. Set your timer for four minutes and make notes about any organizers or storage containers you think you might need for the bathroom.

Then set the timer again for six minutes and do a general pickup of anything that needs to be put away, hung or thrown in the laundry basket. Remove any coffee mugs or dishes that might have collected in the bathroom.

If you've used your bathroom as an extra closet and this project takes you longer than 10 minutes, just pick up where you left off in another session.

Once you've organized random items, you can start on the specific sections of the room.

Section 1: Bathroom Surfaces

Start cleaning the bathroom surfaces by moving left to right around the room. One of your sinks is likely the place you'll begin, so set your timer for five minutes and remove everything from around the sink, including soap, toothbrushes and other items. Thoroughly clean the sink and the counter space around the sink. Wipe down the mirror and the faucet.

Set your timer again for five minutes and begin replacing items you must keep on your sink. Remember, the less clutter the better, so if some items can go under the sink, in your medicine cabinet, or in the linen closet, put them in there for now.

In the next 10-minute session, move to the next surface (another sink, the tub, the toilet area), following the same process of clearing, cleaning, sorting and discarding. If there is anything to donate or move to another room, put these items in the appropriate boxes.

Bathroom Surface Tips:

- Depending on the size of the counter space, consider just leaving out your soap container or soap dish, a small jewelry box and your daily perfume or cologne. Your toothbrush, razor and other personal items should be out of sight. Be sure you store your toothbrush upright in a cup so it can dry out after each use.

- If you use bar soap to wash your hands, consider replacing it with liquid soap. Not only is liquid soap less messy, but germs can grow on bar soap and easily spread from one person to another. Consider getting a decorative soap dispenser and buying a large container of liquid soap to use for refills.

- If you use your tub regularly to bathe and wash your hair, get a tub organizer to hang over the side, or buy a decorative shelf to put on the wall that holds your supplies. If you have a lot of space around the tub, use a decorative basket or other container to hold your stuff. Barrie has a small table next to the tub to hold body wash, bath salts and other bathing necessities.

- If you keep children's bath toys in the tub, put them in a mesh bag, crate or even a colander so they drain after each bath.

- Barrie likes to decorate her bathtub area with scented candles, plants and a stack of pretty towels. You can also install a towel rack on the wall near the tub to hang your towels.

- If your shower is in your tub, you can use a hanging rack over the showerhead to store your shampoos and cleansers.

- If you keep books and magazines near the toilet, you can find a combo toilet paper holder and magazine rack that keeps everything neat and organized.

Section 2: The Shower

Now that you've decluttered all of the surface areas, it's time to hop in the shower. Set your timer for five minutes and remove everything from the shower. Since items might be wet, have a towel handy where you can place the bottles, soaps and razors. Thoroughly clean the shower and wipe down the shower door.

Set the timer again for five minutes and sort through all of the bottles, razors, cleansers and soaps. Throw away any empties, as well as old razors and broken soap pieces. Consolidate any bottles if possible. Wipe down the bottles to remove excess gunk from the outside. Then replace the items you want to keep in the shower.

Shower Tips:

- Keep a squeegee and a bottle of cleaning spray in the shower to give it a quick clean after every shower.
- If you don't have one, get a shower caddy or standing shower butler for storing your toiletries in the shower.
- Want to get rid of all the shampoo, soap and conditioner bottles altogether? If so, invest in a mounted dispenser unit. It lets you squeeze the liquids into the different chambers; then you can pump out a bit at a time.
- For men, if you shave in the shower, invest in a lighted, no-fog mirror with suction cups to mount on the wall.

Women who shave their legs in the shower might want to invest in a mounted foot pedestal.

Section 3: Under the Sink

Now it's time to go *down under*. Let's get that jumbled area under the sink really cleared out and organized. This project will be similar to organizing the area under the kitchen sink. You have the pipes to contend with, but fortunately no disposal, so you have a bit more room here. If you have two sinks, this project might require more than one 10-minute session.

Set your timer for four minutes and pull out everything under the sink. Thoroughly clean the area under the sink and put down waterproof shelf liner if necessary.

Set the timer again for six minutes and begin sorting the items under the sink. Toss anything that is a few years old, useless or has a past-due expiration date. If some items need to go in another spot in the bathroom, go ahead and put them in the right place. If you need to move items to another room, put them in the appropriate box. If you see anything worth giving away, put these in your donation box.

Group like items together and begin placing them back under the sink, with the most-used items toward the front. Make note of any organizers or containers that might be useful here. (See the tips below for ideas.)

Under the Sink Tips:

- Mount an inexpensive wire rack on the inside of the cabinet door for your most-used items, or cut a shoe bag in half and mount it on the cabinet door to hold bottles and small items.
- Stackable bins or baskets can help you keep all of the items under the sink organized and grouped properly—and will help keep spills and leaks off the inside of the cabinet.
- Pull-out shelves are another great option for storage.
- Cut PVC pipe mounted to the inside of the cabinet door is an inexpensive way to store blow dryers, curling irons and their attached cords.
- If you have a lot of small containers and items under the sink, use a lazy Susan so they don't get lost in the bottom of a bin.
- Decorative jars or even canning jars are perfect for storing cotton balls, hair clips and Q-tips.
- If you have a pedestal sink with no storage underneath, you can use baskets, storage towers and other freestanding drawer and shelf units. Here are some great ideas on Pinterest.

Section 4: Medicine Cabinet

Your next project is to go through the medicine cabinet(s). You should be able to easily clear and clean this space in 10 minutes for each cabinet.

Set your timer for four minutes and remove everything from the cabinet. Thoroughly clean the inside and outside of the cabinet. Set the timer again for six minutes and begin sorting through the items. Go through any medications, check expiration dates and toss ones that are outdated. Remember, with medicines that don't have an expiration date, unless you know you purchased them within the past year, it's best to toss them.

Throw out anything else you don't use or that appears old. Old makeup should be thrown out. Here's a general rule of thumb for how long to keep makeup items:

- **Mascara and liquid eyeliner**: When you put the wand back into the tube, you bring in bacteria. Replace every three to four months.
- **Liquid foundation**: Foundation can remain stable for up to a year if kept in a cool, dry place.
- **Lip gloss and lipstick**: These are less likely to grow bacteria. You can hold on to gloss for at least six months and lipstick for a year.

- **Powders**: You can safely use powder-based products for eighteen months to two years.

Medicine Cabinet Tips:

According to the CDC, "more than 60,000 young children go to the emergency room each year because they got into medicines while their parents or caregivers were not looking."

If you have small children, consider removing all prescription and over-the-counter medications from the medicine cabinet and putting them where children can't reach. A locked area is ideal.

Use the medicine cabinet to store the small items you need daily so they don't sit on the counter but are still easily accessible. This might include tweezers, razors, combs, nail clippers, your toothbrush (in a cup or holder), toothpaste, dental floss, contact lens items, shaving cream, face creams and makeup remover.

Rather than keeping medical supplies and bandages in the medicine cabinet, you might want to do what Barrie does and create your own first-aid kit using a plastic bin or basket.

You can add a thermometer, bandages, gauze, rubbing alcohol, adhesive tape, elastic bandages, a syringe or medicine spoon, hydrogen peroxide, antibiotic ointment, calamine lotion and hydrocortisone cream. Depending on where you have room, you can store this in your linen closet, under your sink, in the laundry room or in a kitchen cabinet.

VII

DECLUTTERING YOUR CLOSETS

Section 1: Linen Closets

The main purpose of a linen closet is to store your linens—sheets, blankets and towels. But like most other spaces hidden behind a door, the linen closet gets filled with an assortment of random items that can't be stored anywhere else.

Steve keeps his first-aid kit at the top of the linen closet, along with extra toilet paper, bathroom cleaning supplies, an iron and other bulk extras like shampoo, soap and towels.

It shouldn't take too long to complete the linen closet. The hardest task will be neatly folding those darned fitted sheets that often end up wadded up in your stack of sheets.

Grab your notebook, cleaning supplies and sorting boxes. Set your timer for three minutes and make some notes about how you want to rearrange the closet (see Tips below). Then set the timer again for eight minutes and begin working from top to bottom on the shelves.

Pull everything off the top shelf. Clean the shelf thoroughly. Then begin sorting items to throw away, give away and keep. If you have medications in this closet, don't forget to check expiration dates.

Once you've sorted, return all of the items you want to keep and place the other items in the appropriate boxes. If you have time left, move to the next shelf. If the timer goes off before you finish, just put the items back on the shelf and finish sorting tomorrow.

Continue moving down to the last shelf and the floor under the shelf. Vacuum or clean the floor. Once you finish cleaning and sorting, go back to your sheets and towels and refold them neatly (see Tips below). Then rearrange items on the shelves to your liking.

Linen Closet Tips:

- Place the items you use most on the shelves that are the easier to access. If you have small children, consider putting medications and cleaning products up on a higher shelf.

- Use decorative baskets or plastic bins for storing toilet paper, cleaning supplies and other necessary bathroom products. Group like items together.

- If the entire family shares one linen closet, you might want to dedicate a shelf for the linens and towels for each bedroom and bathroom, labeled with the name of the person occupying the room.

- Folding your sheets isn't as hard as it appears. You just need space to manage that awkward fitted sheet. (Here's a YouTube video on how to fold a fitted sheet—courtesy of Martha Stewart! https://www.youtube.com/watch?v=Q-a2FR1iwqg) Having properly folded sheets will save you a lot of space and look so much neater in your linen closet.

- You can also save space by creating a deep fold for your towels, creating a narrow rectangle rather than a square. (Here's another video on how to do this. https://www.youtube.com/watch?v=C8NTYa5Cf2I)

- You might also consider rolling your towels in tubes and stacking them, which really saves a ton of space and looks very modern.

Section 2: Clothes Closet

As part of her preparation for moving, Barrie recently purged and organized her closet. She got rid of a stack of items (clothes and shoes) she no longer wore, reducing her wardrobe by about a third. She decluttered the closet of miscellaneous items that didn't belong there, tossed out wire hangers and organized everything.

Of all of the decluttering projects she took on as part of her moving project, getting her closet in order felt the most rewarding.

As she says, "There's something very gratifying about walking into your closet and having so much space and organization. It feels like you're walking into the designer area of a women's boutique."

Your clothes are some of the most personal items in your house, and they are a reflection of who you are—your tastes and personal style. Keeping these items neat is a small way of showing respect for yourself.

Depending on how messy your closet is and how many clothes you hang on to, this could be one of the most time-consuming projects. We suggest you begin with a few general sweeps before you really get down to the business of completely sorting and organizing everything. That said, if you have space to hang a lot in your closet, hang as much as possible (of clothes you wear). You tend to wear hanging items more than folded items because you can see the clothes better.

How to Get Started

Grab your notebook, cleaning supplies and sorting boxes and set your timer for six minutes. Use this six minutes to make an initial sweep through all of your clothes and shoes and pull out anything you no longer want to keep. Remember: if it hasn't been worn in a year, or it's tattered, or you simply don't like it, the item should be purged.

After you've made this first sweep, use the remaining time to fold the items and place them in a donation box. If this process takes longer than 10 minutes, break it up into two or more sessions.

Once you make the first sweep of items to give away, set your timer again for five minutes and remove any sweaters or knits. Set your timer again to fold the sweaters and knits, putting them in the appropriate drawers.

Next, make one more sweep of your closet, looking for items that need to be stored elsewhere. Try to use your closet for clothing and clothing-related items only, if possible. Set the timer for six minutes and move left to right through your closet, pulling out these items. Set the timer again for four minutes and place items in "donate," "trash" or "store elsewhere" boxes.

You should have more room in your closet after purging your clothes, shoes and other items. However, if your closet is small and you have a lot of clothes, go back through one more time and remove all of the off-season clothes. Set the timer for six minutes to pull them all out and use the remaining four minutes to either put them in another closet or begin folding them to put in a storage container (more on this in the Tips below). This process of removing and storing off-season clothes may take you more than one 10-minute session.

How to Organize Clothes

Set the timer for 10 minutes and go through the hanging clothes, organizing like items together (e.g., jeans, shirts, jackets and heavy coats). If you have time before the timer goes off, arrange the sorted items by color.

If you have a closet with several heights of hanging rods or wire racks, arrange clothing so the longer items, like dresses and coats, don't touch the floor or the rod or rack below.

Use another 10-minute session to get rid of all wire and dry-cleaning hangers and put all of your clothes (or as many as possible) on matching hangers. If you prefer to hang your pants at their full length, you can use wooden clamp hangers.

How to Organize Shoes

If possible, keep everything off the closet floor to keep it looking spacious and neat. That includes your shoes.

Again, if you are in need of space, use a 10-minute project to remove off-season shoes to store elsewhere. Use another 10-minute project to put your shoes on a shoe rack or in a bin. Here are some other creative ways to store shoes.

How to Organize Other Items

Your closet might still have items like hats, purses, belts, ties or even suitcases. Set your timer for 10 minutes and move through your closet again, placing anything you use infrequently on the highest shelves. Sort like items together and place items you use frequently within easy reach.

Finish by Cleaning Your Closet

Take 10 minutes to do a final cleaning of your closet, if necessary. Sweep, dust and/or vacuum the floor, remove any trash and take any dirty clothes to the laundry room.

Clothes Closet Tips:

- Never leave your dresses, suits or any other clothes in dry-cleaning or plastic garment bags. The chemicals from dry cleaning attack the fibers of your clothing and cause damage.

- If your closet is small, optimize the space by using a single hanger for two pieces of clothing. Use clip-ons to hold skirts neatly, or hang two pair of jeans on one hanger.
- If you keep all of your clothes for every season in one closet, organize the clothes seasonally with different colored hangers. For example, use yellow hangers for summer, red for fall, white for winter and green for spring.
- Use notched hangers for items with thin straps, such as lingerie or spaghetti-strap dresses.
- Use suit hangers with non-slip bars for the pants to hang your suits neatly.
- Use sturdy pant hangers to hang your boots and keep them off the floor.
- Double the hanging space by hooking one hanger over another.
- If you wear a lot of jeans, save space by using shower hooks to hang jeans by a belt loop instead of using a hanger.
- For women, organize your shoes with the right shoe toe out and left shoe heel out so you can see the back and front of the shoe to help you plan what to wear.
- Use vertical space (both above and below the closet rod) to store more, using rolling bins, dividers and stackable towers. You can use these for folded items such as sweaters, jeans and scarves.
- Use hooks on the back of the closet door (or an over-the-door hanging unit) to hang belts, scarves and other accessories.
- Store off-season clothing in space-saving vacuum storage bags, under your bed in containers or in decorative baskets with lids that pull double-duty as furniture.
- Use cut PVC for storing scarves, belts or ties in drawers.

- Use a bulletin board on the wall of your closet to hang earrings, necklaces and other jewelry for easy access. Here are 34 other ideas for storing jewelry: http://bit.ly/1Hqt4TR
- Use clear, stackable shoe boxes to easily see your shoes and keep them dust-free.
- Consider putting a handbag organizer on a closet shelf to keep your purses on display.
- The best way to store men's ties is to unknot them and drape them over a prong on a tie rack immediately after you wear them. The next best way to store ties is by rolling them loosely and putting them in a box or drawer.
- Continue the purging process throughout the year by turning your hanger backward every time you wear something. In a year, go through your closet again and get rid of anything with an unturned hanger.

VIII

DECLUTTER YOUR KID'S ROOMS

Introduction

Decluttering your children's rooms presents more than an opportunity for another tidy space. It gives you the opportunity to teach your children valuable life skills, increase their creativity and imagination, and even improve their social and intellectual development.

As parents, we want the best for our children, and we often believe giving them more "stuff" is a sign of how much we love them. However, there's a diminishing point of return with toys and other possessions. Research has shown children lose the ability to play properly for their ideal development when given too many toys.

In a study funded by the National Center for Infants, Toddlers, and Families, childhood development researcher Claire Lerner said: "Our studies show that giving children too many toys, or toys of the wrong type, can actually be doing them harm. They become overwhelmed and cannot concentrate on any one thing long enough to learn from it."

This study is supported by other research, including a study conducted by Kathy Sylva, professor of educational psychology at Oxford University in the UK. She says, "When they have a large number of toys there seems to be a distraction element and when children are distracted they do not learn or play well."

Claire Learner suggests keeping four or five toys out at a time and perhaps rotating toys based on your child's interests and temperament.

By cutting back on the number of toy options and selecting toys that promote problem-solving skills, social interaction and creative expression, you allow your child to engage with the remaining toys on a deeper and more creative level. As a side benefit, fewer toys reduces the amount of conflict among siblings.

By purging your child's toys, you can also teach your kids valuable lessons about sharing with other children, being mindful about spending and keeping their rooms organized.

Get Started by Sorting Toys

When Barrie's children were young, she helped them declutter (during the holiday season) by asking them to select several toys and books to eliminate. Then her children would wrap their toys and take them to a needy family.

Children have a tremendous capacity for compassion. If your child is willing to purge some of their own toys in this way, you are off to a great start with decluttering and engaging them in the process. If you see other toys that go unnoticed or rarely used in their rooms, take a 10-minute session to include them in your donation box.

Next, use one or two 10-minute sessions to ask your child to select 15 to 20 favorite toys and books. These are the toys you can rotate in their rooms (five or six at a time) over the next few weeks or months. Put these toys and books in a basket or on a shelf for them to see and access easily.

After you've narrowed down the toys your child wants to give away and decided what will be kept in the room, sort the remaining items. This should be done when your child isn't around, as they'll likely suddenly become attached to a toy that is about to disappear.

Grab your empty boxes and set your timer for 10 minutes. During this time, simply gather all of the remaining toys and put them in the boxes. Take the boxes to another room, out of your child's sight, to sort them.

Use one or more 10-minute sessions to go through these toys and throw away any that are broken or have missing pieces. Then select any additional toys and books that can be donated. After that, sort the toys by type or category in storage bins and label the bins. Finally, store the bins in your basement, storage room, garage or a closet your kids can't access.

As your child grows disinterested with the toys in their room, pull others from the boxes and swap them out. This way, you keep the number of toys to a minimum and your children don't feel overwhelmed with a vast array of items in their rooms.

Other Decluttering

Once the toys and books are sorted and purged, start decluttering the rest of the room. Grab your notebook, boxes and timer. Again, get your child engaged in the process with you. Ten minutes isn't a long time even for a preschooler. They can help you make the bed, pick up laundry, sort clothing items in boxes and help with simple cleaning.

Begin each 10-minute task by making the bed, as you did with your own room. Talk to your child about the importance of making the bed first thing after they awaken. This is a great time to help them establish this lifelong habit.

Follow the same process you did with your own room, starting with basic clutter (aside from toys), cleaning surface areas and organizing each drawer. Once you finish the room, use a 10-minute session to dust and vacuum.

Kid's Room Tips:

- Once you select the toys to keep in your child's room, be sure to disinfect them—especially if your child has been sick or others have recently played there. This minimizes the spread of germs to other family members.
- Big items, like dollhouses and train sets, take up a lot of space. If your child's room is small, these might need to go to a different location or be donated, especially if they're rarely used.

- Put a note on your calendar to rotate toys and games periodically. Your kids will be thrilled when they rediscover toys they haven't seen in a while.

- Help your child select toys that inspire creativity, problem solving and interaction with others. Look for toys that can be used in multiple ways (e.g., blocks, Legos, puppets, dress-up clothes or play kitchens).

- Barrie had a craft area for her kids in their rooms and encouraged them to spend daily time on creative efforts. This area should have a good-sized work surface, ample lighting and organized supplies.

- Clothing can be a big contributor to a disorganized bedroom. Be sure to eliminate outgrown clothes on a regular basis and put a laundry hamper or basket in your child's room for dirty clothes. Teach your kids how to fold and hang clothes and make a "no clothes touch the floor" rule.

- Hang your child's pants and coordinating shirts together on one hanger, or put them together in a large freezer bag in a dresser drawer. This makes it easier for children to pick out their own clothing and get dressed in the morning. You can even label these outfits by days of the week.

- Use a Tupperware container or box with an attached lid to store small items like doll accessories. The attached lid helps you maintain all of the small bits and pieces.

- If you decide to keep more than a few toys and games in your child's room, use clear plastic bins to store them so your child can easily see what's inside. Shallow (rather than deep) containers make it easier to find items. You can use a shelving unit or cabinet to store the bins. For toddlers and younger children, keep the bins out of their reach so you can pull them down and contain the mess.

- Another way to organize toys is to make some of them accessible in different rooms. You might have a few toys and games in your children's bedrooms and a few in the family room or another designated play area.

- Older children and teenagers are able to clean and organize their own rooms without your assistance. Teach them the 10-minute room decluttering process you use and ensure they work on their rooms for 10 minutes a day until the process is complete. Then maintain the 10-minute habit every evening before bed so they can keep their rooms clean.

IX

DECLUTTER THE FAMILY ROOM

Introduction

The family room shouldn't take too much time. Usually this area contains a few pieces of furniture, an entertainment center, a coffee table and a few assorted items, so the process for decluttering it will be similar to what you do in the bedroom and your kids' rooms.

To get started, you need a few items: multiple boxes, garbage bags and labels. Once you're ready, set the timer for 10 minutes and begin with the furniture.

First, clear everything off your furniture. Here you will go through each item and make quick decisions about what to donate or keep. Identify items that have sentimental value for certain family members and set them aside for the time being. Take items that don't belong in this area (like bills, kitchen items or athletic gear) and move them into the correct room.

Second, throw out anything that's trash or unusable. Put all the items you'll keep in a box until you've completed this mini-project.

This step might be a bit painful. Odds are, you'll have to go through these items and make quick decisions about what you really want:

- Toys
- DVDs, even VHS tapes
- Video games
- Children's books

- Old magazines
- Assorted knick-knacks

As always, if an item hasn't been used in the last year, give it away.

Go through everything in the room to determine whether it needs to stay there. For all the remaining items, ask whether anyone has used them in the last year. If the answer is no, throw them away, give them away, donate them or recycle them. If an item doesn't fit with your overall plan for the space, find it a home in another room where it will be more suitable.

Next, clean all the furniture. You'll follow a pattern similar to the one you used to clean the rest of your home—wipe down surfaces, vacuum between the crevices, dust all electronics and organize all of the wires.

Finally, let family members keep some items in this room. Simply assign each person a specific area where they can keep their possessions. If they have too many items, ask them to move them to their bedrooms or eliminate what they no longer use.

Family Room Tips

- Consider buying organizational tools that will be the designated spot for certain items. You might put a tray by your chair for the newspaper or buy a wicker basket for toys. Make sure family members know the designated spot for each item.
- Purchase furniture that has extra storage space, such as a coffee table with baskets or a couch with a storage area.
- Consider digital versions of movies and music. Nowadays, most entertainment can be streamed through your TV (via services like Hulu or Netflix) If you love watching *Super Troopers* every month, you can access that movie (and thousands more) with a simple subscription.
- Use woven baskets for large items. Not only do these baskets add a touch of class to the family room, they also

serve as large containers for the items you choose to keep.

- The family room is often a common area used by everyone. This means everyone should have a vote and opinion on how this room looks. Even though your ultimate goal is to create a clutter-free environment, be sure to get feedback instead of making unilateral decisions.

X

DECLUTTERING YOUR OFFICE

Introduction

Your bedroom and office are the two areas where you spend the most time. Think of it this way: if you average eight hours of work and eight hours of sleep every day, that means almost two-thirds of your life is spent in these two spaces. This makes it just as important to declutter your office as it is to declutter the rest of your home.

Your office is your place of business. And since you are cleaning a professional area, why not treat it in a professional manner? This area should *only* contain items that relate to your business and create a productive mindset. In this section, we'll show you how to do this.

Getting Started with Your Office

The size of this decluttering task can vary depending on whether you have a large home office or a small cubicle at work.

Your first job is to determine the difficulty of the task and make a plan. Start by asking a few questions:

- What do you desire from your office?
- What does it currently lack?
- What can you (immediately) remove from the room?
- What problems do you foresee with making changes in the office?
- What do you need to do (every day) to maintain a decluttered space?

- What aspect of office organization matters most to you?

Don't do this in your head. *Write down* the answers. This gives you time to think over what you really want from this space. You'll use these responses to create an action plan for tackling your office. Then you can get started.

Divide Your Workspace into Zones

Typically, an office has many individual "zones." (This is often true even when working in a compressed cubicle.)

- An area for work with a computer, keyboard, mouse and/or tablet
- A library for research, even if it is simply a few important books and/or manuals
- A storage area for supplies
- An area for incoming and outgoing paperwork
- A filing area for paperwork archives

The object here is to declutter on an area-by-area basis. Like each section of your home, you'll organize one complete area before moving on to the next one.

Section 1: Office Desk

This section is for tackling the space that's used the most—your office desk.

It is a simple 10-minute task to do this. Get a box and put everything currently on your desk into the box, except for the mouse, keyboard and computer.

Now with everything off your desk, use your cleaning supplies to give the entire area a good scrub down. Once it's clean and empty, begin the rest of the process of decluttering your office.

Office Desk Tips

- Your desk should contain what you use on a daily basis. Generally speaking, this means only computer equipment, pen, paper and your calendar. Everything else will be stored in the organized sections that we'll discuss throughout this chapter.

- One way to ensure you have a decluttered desk is to sit in your chair and extend your arms. The spaces within your "wingspan" should contain only the items used on a daily basis. Everything else should be organized or filed away.

- You can keep personal items on your desk (like photos or a sentimental item), but try not to overload the area with random knick-knacks.

- Notes for meetings clutter your space, so be sure to create a daily process where you make decisions on what to do with this paperwork (we'll talk more about this in a bit).
- Move your printer and/or scanner off your desk. These are bulky items that aren't typically used on a daily basis. Put them under your desk or in another location in your office.

Section 2: Electronics

Monitors, keyboards and other electronics can quickly become grungy looking. Since you're decluttering your office, why not take time to clean these as well? This is another perfect 10-minute task because it only takes a short bit of time to go through all your items.

Use compressed air to spray any dust, crumbs and debris out of your keyboard. Then wipe down all flat surfaces (except for screens) on the keyboard, desktop, phone and printer with a lint-free rag.

To do a thorough job, take a Q-tip and clean all the cracks between the keys. You'll probably need a few Q-tips because a lot of stuff can get in there.

For your computer screens, you'll probably need a special LCD cleaning solution that won't damage the screen or leave streaks. You can get this in a spray or sometimes as little pre-moistened towelettes.

Electronic Tips:

- Consider using twist-ties and labels for all your wires. Not only will this make them look more presentable, it will also help you identify where each item connects.
- Cleaning electronics is an ongoing project, so be sure to set aside a few minutes each week to clean the electronics in your office.

Section 3: Desk Drawers

All the junk that's cleared off your desktop will need to go somewhere. That usually means the items will end up in your desk drawer. The trick is to avoid the common mistake most people make: taking everything and dumping it into a single drawer. All this does is create a disorganized mess that has a negative impact on your productivity.

You can organize desk drawers by grouping items together. (For instance, here's a Pinterest photo of a well-organized drawer.)

That said, you shouldn't be obsessive about finding a container for everything. The important thing is to focus on the items you use most often. Pens need to be next to pens, paperclips next to paperclips and so forth.

There are many ways to be creative when organizing similar items. There are many organizational products made specifically for desks. You can try plastic inserts, or you can use a nice wooden drawer.

For every desk drawer, consider doing four separate tasks (if you're dealing with a lot of items):

1. Spend the first 10 minutes emptying the drawer, placing everything into a box (or in the case of small items like paperclips, setting them aside to be grouped later), and then thoroughly cleaning the inside of the drawer.

2. Make (or buy) inserts to segregate all items within the drawer.
3. Put back the office supplies you use on a regular basis (like pens, pencils, paperclips, tape and scissors). Keep anything you're not sure about in the box.
4. After 30 days, if anything is still in the box, then consider these items to be junk. Give them away or throw them out. If something isn't used in the span of a month, then you really don't need it.

Desk Drawer Tips:

*   You can get creative with drawers by crafting cardboard inserts. Steve has seen tuna cans, egg cartons, mason jars and all sorts of "repurposed" items that have been used for desk drawer organization.
*   Be sure to put any loose change into a coin drawer. You can save up this money and go to a Coinstar machine to redeem it for a gift certificate.
*   Take time to tightly cap any liquid items (like Wite-Out).
*   Test any batteries to make sure they're still functional. If not, put them in a recycling box.

Section 4: Active Paperwork

Paperwork is the lifeblood of most businesses, so the area where the paperwork flows in and out is the heart of the office.

The problem is that paperwork accounts for the largest amount of clutter in any office. It often crowds your desktop, table, shelves, drawers, file cabinet and even the floor. That's why it's not surprising that many people have trouble finding the right documents in an expedient manner.

For some, the solution is to go paperless, but even that can be a challenge because you need a system for scanning and filing these digital files.

The best solution for many people is to create a daily system for their documents. Not only will this organize your existing paperwork, it will help you process paper as it comes in.

The obvious first step is to tackle your inbox and outbox. Most people have trays for incoming and outgoing mail. Unfortunately, it's not easy to use these items effectively. In this section, we'll map out a process for creating a paperwork system that works.

Organizing Your Paperwork

Before we get into the "how-to" process, it's important to understand the distinct lifecycle of paperwork:

1. Paperwork comes into the office. It's delivered by your boss, co-worker or the postal service. It also comes in the form of printed email, documents handed out during meetings and printouts from websites.
2. Paperwork is sorted according to what needs to be done. Things that require work go in one pile. Bills go in another. Tasks to be completed are placed in another and "archived" items go in the final pile.
3. Paperwork is processed. Whatever "action" is needed is accomplished.
4. Paper is stored, destroyed or sent elsewhere.

These four steps form the basics of how paperwork is usually handled. The key to managing your documents is to take action based on the *type* of paperwork and where it is in the lifecycle.

First off, your physical inbox should only contain pieces of paper that don't have specific actions assigned to them. At the end of every workday, this inbox should be emptied. This doesn't mean the work has been completed, but you've at least given the paper a new "home."

Next, you should file these items in multiple folders (preferably multicolored) based on the action that's needed. Simply break them down according to the following:

*   Read and sign
*   Bills
*   Write back (correspondence)
*   Call
*   Read (informational only)
*   Action needed
*   Task oriented (If you have major projects, I would recommend a folder for each.)

Processing paperwork can become a major obstacle to creating an efficient inbox system. Many people leave papers in their inboxes (or scattered around tables) as they deal with the different tasks. However, if you file papers in separate folders, you can quickly organize paper according to what needs to be done.

Streamlining your work based on actions makes things more efficient. Rather than constantly shifting gears as you work, focus on similar tasks in bulk before moving on to the next action that needs attention.

Next, there should be an area in your office for a filing cabinet, flip folders or file boxes. The amount of space you need varies by how much paperwork you handle on a daily basis. With more of the world going paperless, this filing system *could* be kept to a single cabinet or drawer.

This system can be organized in any way that makes sense to you. The important thing is to have a consistent process so you can quickly store paperwork and get it off your desk.

You shouldn't keep every single piece of paper that you come across. Most papers can be destroyed or thrown away. Anything with personal information should be shredded. We recommend keeping a shredder under your desk so you can destroy unimportant items as you sort and process.

Paperwork Tips:

- Create a good filing system for all paperwork. This means having a separate folder for each of the following: finances, insurance, taxes, utilities, warranties, school documents and health records. You can even narrow down each of these categories based on the number of documents you receive on a regular basis.

- Invest in a filing cabinet, plus hanging file dividers and manila folders. This will display all your files in an organized way so you can quickly retrieve any item.

- Another option is to use a wall organizer for these items or a partitioned box for all active paperwork.

- Maintain small storage boxes for each year. For instance, you probably know it's important to keep tax records for the past seven years. By having a box for each year, you can toss out paperwork from the oldest box, rewrite the label and then include documents from the past year.

Section 5: Scan Your Paperwork (Optional)

In the last section, we sidetracked from the "10-minute declutter" process to discuss a specific solution for decreasing general office clutter. Now it is time to step back into our imaginary office and get back to organizing everything.

Depending on how long you've stored paperwork, you may have a massive number of documents or perhaps very little.

There is really nothing "wrong" with having a lot of paper (if you can immediately find specific documents). The only downside is you'll need multiple filing cabinets that can take up a lot of space.

Our question to you is:

"How much paper do you really need?"

Odds are, you probably keep more than you need.

Use a high-speed scanner (like the NeatDesk or the CamScanner mobile app) to quickly decrease the amount of paper clutter.

If you have a multi-folder filing system, the best way to handle this may be working on a single folder at a time. This task is perfect for one 10-minute decluttering session—work on one folder during one session. If some of your folders are pretty thin, you might be able to work through a few at a time.

Scanning Tips

- Be ruthless with your documents. Even with a high-speed scanner, the project will take a long time if you try to digitize each document. We recommend you eliminate needless items first and *then* scan everything else.

- Keep only the *most important* paperwork—like items stored for legal or tax purposes. Everything else can be scanned and saved to a program like Evernote. With this program, you can add tags and descriptions to make finding information far easier than you could if it was stored in a physical folder.

- Sign up for online statements. Most companies now offer digital versions of their paperwork (like bank statements, utility bills and credit card statements). Sign up and save yourself the hassle of having to digitize these documents.

- Use a service like Catalog Choice to get rid of junk mail. The fewer items you receive, the more time you'll have to focus on important documents.

- Once you've minimized the amount of mail you receive, you can use a service like Earth Class Mail to digitize the rest.

Section 6: Cables and Cords

Technology is great, but it can also cause a lot of clutter—especially when you're buried under cables and cords. Not only can they be unsightly, they also can be unsafe. The simplest solution is to take a few 10-minute blocks to organize all the cords in your office.

Zip ties are your best friend. A few well-placed zip ties can secure your cables, eliminating trip hazards and reducing the likelihood that your cables will end up in a tangled mess.

Next, label all cables. A little circular tab is easy to place on a cord. Since nearly all electronics cords disconnect at both ends, this will help you find the "correct" cord regardless of how many times you move things around.

Finally, organize unused cords into cubbies where they won't get tangled with other cables.

Cord Tip:

- Use old toilet paper rolls to store cables. (Here's a photo of how this looks: http://bit.ly/1HDAIje)

Section 7: Digital Files

Digital organization goes beyond the scope of this book. In fact, it's a big enough topic that it deserves its own book (perhaps we'll write it one day). But since we're talking about decluttering your office, it's important to briefly cover how to systematize your digital files.

Your digital life is a reflection of your physical life. If you have disorganized chaos in one, odds are you have the same problem with the other. Once your physical area is organized, spend time creating an organizational hierarchy for your digital content.

#1. Create a central location for all your files. You should be able to update and access important files at work, at home or even from your mobile device.

For instance, Steve keeps all his files on <u>Dropbox</u>. You could use this or a few other options to store and back up your digital items:

Some other options:

- Google Drive
- Microsoft OneDrive
- Amazon CloudDrive
- Wuala
- CloudMe
- Box

We live an age where hacking can happen to any of us, so be sure to back up your files on a daily basis. You can use a company like Carbonite to do this automatically.

#2. Set limits on digital time wasters. Social media and funny cat videos can be entertaining, but they eat into your productivity, which leaves you less time to *actually* enjoy your life. Our advice is to use a tool like Rescue Time to monitor how you spend time on your computer during the workday.

#3. Organize files by content, not file type. By default, most systems will place files in folders based on file type, such as pictures in "My Pictures" or documents in "My Documents." This is fine at first, but it can quickly get out of control when you have too many files.

A simple solution is to organize folders (and sub-folders) by the different aspects of your business. That way, you won't jump from folder to folder looking for certain items. When you take the time to create a systematic filing system, you can immediately find the right documents—no matter how many items are on your computer.

As an example, the book you're currently reading is stored in a specific location on Steve's computer:

Main Folder → Develop Good Habits → Kindle Books → 10 Minute Declutter → 10_Minute_Declutter.epub

Create a series of folders like this, and you won't have a problem finding any file on your computer.

#4. Use Evernote to capture ideas. Evernote is great for storing photos, thoughts, websites and quotes—whatever you need for the future should go into this tool. This is a free tool that's perfect for storing and organizing random thoughts in a system that makes everything easy to retrieve.

#5. Limit email. Like walking into a dirty room, seeing a crowded inbox can be a stressful experience. Our advice is to keep your inbox as organized as possible on a daily basis. You don't have to get to "inbox zero" every day, but it's important to put a process in place for organizing the influx of email.

There is a *lot more* you can do to declutter your digital life, but if you complete these five tasks on a daily basis, you'll set the framework for a solid digital filing system.

Section 8: General Office Organization

As we come to the end of this section, we'd like to give a few final tips for decluttering and organizing your office.

General Office Tips:

- Hang hooks or have a coat rack by door. This will keep jackets, purses and umbrellas from cluttering your space.
- Give your desk a left-to-right workflow. Paperwork should come in on the left of your desk; process folders and work files should be in the middle; and storage files should be on the right.
- Business cards no longer need to be stored in a Rolodex. Steve scans business cards in to Evernote and tags them as business cards, making a searchable index of business cards he can find from any platform. There are other methods you can use. There are quite a few smartphone apps designed JUST to be instant Rolodexes. It's easy to find one with a quick search online. Here are a few: CamCard Free, CardToContact or ScanBizCards Lite.
- Organize your desk and drawers in order of importance. Frequently used items should go in the closest drawers with other items stored farther away.
- Limit how many items you keep in your office. Keep one bookshelf or one cabinet, not several of each. If they fill

up, get rid of items you don't use or digitize any unnecessary paperwork.

- Buy bright and colorful artwork for your walls (or get artwork from your kids or grandkids if you have them). This will brighten up your office and make for a more pleasant working environment.

- Every item in your office should have a "home," a desk space, drawer, cabinet or bookshelf where it goes when your office is in its perfectly organized condition.

- Mark all appointments on your calendar of choice. Don't leave a bunch of Post-it notes scattered around because this will only create more clutter. Use a digital calendar app like QuickCal or Google Calendar to keep track of every scheduled appointment.

- Get a small plant, flowers or a fern for your office, something to "green" up the place and make it a homier and less antiseptic environment. Remember, you will spend up to a third of your time here, so make it nice.

XI

DECLUTTERING YOUR GARAGE/BASEMENT

Introduction

We decided to group the basement and garage together because many people treat these areas as storage for items that shouldn't kept anywhere else. This can include anything from kitchen goods and lawn items to seasonal decorations and power tools.

Unfortunately, it's easy to treat these areas like a dumping ground for items that *should be* organized or eliminated. Many homeowners put their possessions in the garage or basement with an "out of sight, out of mind" approach. Over time, clutter accumulates, making it difficult to go in and out of the garage or access the items you have stored in the basement.

There is a good chance your garage or basement is full of items you no longer need. Even though this is the final section of the book, it might take the longest time to declutter these areas because you've probably accumulated a lot of stuff over the past few years. Let's get to it.

Planning Your Garage and Basement Decluttering Project

The secret to keeping these areas organized is to make use of wall space. Instead of throwing everything into a jumbled mess, use shelves to organize like items together.

You can find quality shelves at any home improvement store or on Amazon. If you're good with woodworking, you can make your own.

Keep records of where major items are stored (or at least have a general idea of the location of each item). An easy way to do this is to number shelves and boxes for easy retrieval. That way, you can look at your list and know that Christmas lights are "Shelf 3, Box H." Yes, this will take extra work, but it will save you a lot of time when you don't have to search through box after box.

Third, put all "like items" in boxes or on numbered shelves according to the season (i.e., Christmas decorations, spring gardening tools or snow-removal items.) If possible, put these items into clear plastic tubs so you can easily locate them when needed.

Don't store things your family doesn't need or use. Sure, some items are seasonal, but if you haven't used something in three years, then it's time to get rid of it. Your garage and basement should be a place to store important tools, not hide your hoarding.

Finally, keep a shelf for empty buckets, trash bags and containers. When you start to purge the basement and garage, these items will be very useful.

Now, let's dive into a lengthy project you'll need to complete to declutter both your garage and basement.

Decluttering Your Garage (and Basement)

When you declutter your basement and garage, you'll follow a pattern similar to the process you used to declutter the rest of your home. Once you find a process that works for you, it's easy to apply the process to other areas of the house. We'll explain how to declutter your garage and then you can apply the same process to decluttering your basement.

Decluttering your garage is one project where it makes sense to do everything in a single day. You're pulling items out of your garage, and you don't want to leave them lying around.

We suggest you do this project on a sunny or rain-free day. Why? Because most of your things will end up outdoors as you sort your stuff into piles to keep, throw, move, donate, toss or sell.

It's best to set aside part of a day (like a Saturday) to declutter your garage and then put the items back in.

Get started by pulling everything out of your garage. This includes gardening equipment, yard items, storage boxes and athletic gear. If you're like most people, you will put these items in your driveway or the grass next to it. If the garage is *really* full, then do one area at a time.

Once you've cleared everything out, clean the inside of your garage. This task includes wiping down dirt surfaces, cleaning cobwebs, sweeping out dirt and emptying out flowerpots. Spend an hour or two on this task because it's probably been a few years since you've cleared this area.

Third, install peg boards, nails or hooks on your garage walls. These tools free up floor space and make it easy to grab the item you need. Be sure to use garbage bags, boxes, labels, markers and other organizational tools.

Now you'll begin the process of decluttering your garage. Start two piles—one for items you'll keep and the other for items you want to discard. Use the same rule of thumb we've followed throughout this book—if you haven't used an item in the last few years, then get rid of it.

After that, clean the items you decided to keep. This will be similar to what you did with the garage interior—clean off dust, dirt and cobwebs. Wipe down the surfaces of any tools, such as a lawnmower or cutting saw.

Finally, once your items have been decluttered and cleaned, group them together in a way that makes sense to you.

For instance, you might decide to put related seasonal items in the same location. One area could have deicing salt and snow shovels, and another would have pots, soil and gardening equipment. With this type of organization, you can quickly find items based on their purpose.

Garage/Basement Tips:

- You might need to recruit friends and family for this project because you will probably have to move heavy items.
- Rent a dumpster if you know you're going to be throwing away a lot of junk (simply go to Google Maps and enter the keyword phrase "dumpster rental" to find one near you).
- Install a fold-down table for when you want to do a home project (like potting plants). You'll get more space and still have a place for working on random tasks.
- Create a system for athletic gear. If you (or your family members) have a lot of athletic activities, you can get

overwhelmed by bats, balls, rackets, clubs, skis and various footgear. The simplest solution is to set up racks and shelves for this gear. Just use this search on Pinterest to get a few ideas. (http://bit.ly/1cdk8IQ)

- Paint should not be stored in a garage because it's a hazardous material that should be kept in a cool, dry place like your basement. Also, you can't throw it away. You either have to drop it off at a hazardous waste plant or use the Paint Care website to find a location near you.

- Be careful with storing certain items in your garage. Canned food can spoil in the heat, gas grills require ventilation and electronics can get damaged from exposure to extreme temperatures. Take a few minutes to make sure it's safe to store certain items in the garage or basement.

- Hooks can help you maximize space in these areas. For instance, HGTV has a 15-photo spread that showcases how simple hooks can help you create a well-organized garage.

Final Thoughts...

You should now have a firm grasp of what it takes to declutter your home in 10-minute blocks—*even* if you have a crazy-busy schedule.

Now, before you go, we would like to reinforce three important points:

#1. Commit to 10 Minutes Daily

The premise of this book is simple—you can declutter a home *if* you commit to a 10-minute habit. It's okay to do more if you have the time, but it's more important to stick with a daily schedule.

The secret to habit development isn't how much (or how long) you do an activity. Instead, it's all about consistency. We recommend you review the 8 Steps to Form the Declutter Habit section a few times. Then find a way to fit the declutter routine into your schedule.

#2. Start with the Right Supplies

You can waste a lot of time driving back and forth for decluttering products. A simpler solution is to purchase what you need ahead of time. As mentioned before, we have a simple shopping list of products you can get from Amazon: http://www.developgoodhabits.com/decluttering-supply-list/

That said, since this is a book on decluttering, it wouldn't be right to suggest that you "need" every possible cleaning item.

You'll end up purchasing things that will go to waste. Our suggestion is to focus on the first room and purchase what you'll need for that. Then repeat this process until you have only the items you need to declutter every room in your home.

#3. Tackle Your Favorite Rooms First

We are all motivated by results. When you see the positive benefits of an action, it's more likely you'll continue to do it. This also applies to decluttering your home. When you're constantly reminded of your progress, you'll feel more inspired to keep doing it.

Our recommendation is to start with the rooms where you spend the most time, such as your bedroom, office, bathrooms and family room. Once these areas are organized, you'll create a space that makes you feel relaxed. This is an important feeling to have when you're tackling projects that are not fun—like removing cobwebs and dirt from a cluttered garage.

Well, we've reached the end of this book. You now know how to create a consistent decluttering habit and how to get started.

As always, Steve wants to reinforce the idea of taking action. All the information in this book is worthless *unless* you do something with it. We urge you to schedule a time each day for your habit, grab a few basic supplies, pick a room where you spend the most time and then get started.

It's not hard to declutter your life—all you need is 10 minutes a day to make it happen!

We wish you all the best.

Barrie Davenport

www.liveboldandbloom.com

Steve "S.J." Scott

www.DevelopGoodHabits.com

Did You Like 10-Minute Declutter?

Before you go, we'd like to say "thank you" for purchasing our book.

You could have picked from dozens of books on habit development, but you took a chance and checked out this one.

So a big thanks for purchasing this book and reading all the way to the end.

Now we'd like ask for a *small* favor. **Could you please take a minute or two and leave a review for this book on Amazon?**

This feedback will help us continue to write the kind of books that help you get results. And if you loved it, then please let us know. :-)

More Books by Barrie

- *Self-Discovery Questions: 155 Breakthrough Questions to Accelerate Massive Action*

- *Sticky Habits: 6 Simple Steps To Create Good Habits That Stick*

- *Peace of Mindfulness: Everyday Rituals to Conquer Anxiety and Claim Unlimited Inner Peace*

- *Confidence Hacks: 99 Small Actions to Massively Boost Your Confidence*

- *Building Confidence: Get Motivated, Overcome Social Fear, Be Assertive, and Empower Your Life For Success*

- *The 52-Week Life Passion Project: Uncover Your Life Passion*

More Books by Steve

- *Exercise Every Day: 32 Tactics for Building the Exercise Habit (Even If You Hate Working Out)*

- *The Daily Entrepreneur: 33 Success Habits for Small Business Owners, Freelancers and Aspiring 9-to-5 Escape Artists*

- *Master Evernote: The Unofficial Guide to Organizing Your Life with Evernote (Plus 75 Ideas for Getting Started)*

- *Bad Habits No More: 25 Steps to Break ANY Bad Habit*

- *Habit Stacking: 97 Small Life Changes That Take Five Minutes or Less*

- *To-Do List Makeover: A Simple Guide to Getting the Important Things Done*

- *23 Anti-Procrastination Habits: How to Stop Being Lazy and Get Results in Your Life*

- *S.M.A.R.T. Goals Made Simple: 10 Steps to Master Your Personal and Career Goals*

- *115 Productivity Apps to Maximize Your Time: Apps for iPhone, iPad, Android, Kindle Fire and PC/iOS Desktop Computers*

- *Writing Habit Mastery: How to Write 2,000 Words a Day and Forever Cure Writer's Block*

- *Daily Inbox Zero: 9 Proven Steps to Eliminate Email Overload*

- *Wake Up Successful: How to Increase Your Energy and Achieve Any Goal with a Morning Routine*

- *10,000 Steps Blueprint: The Daily Walking Habit for Healthy Weight Loss and Lifelong Fitness*

- *70 Healthy Habits: How to Eat Better, Feel Great, Get More Energy and Live a Healthy Lifestyle*

- *Resolutions That Stick! How 12 Habits Can Transform Your New Year*

All books can be found at: www.developgoodhabits.com

About the Authors

S.J. Scott

In his books, S.J. Scott provides daily action plans for every area of your life: health, fitness, work and personal relationships. Unlike other personal development guides, his content focuses on taking action. So instead of reading over-hyped strategies that rarely work in the real-world, you'll get information that can be immediately implemented.

Barrie Davenport

Barrie is the founder of an award-winning personal development site, Live Bold and Bloom (liveboldandbloom.com). She is a certified personal coach and online course creator, helping people apply practical, evidence-based solutions and strategies to push past comfort zones and create happier, richer, more successful lives. She is also the author of a series of self-improvement books on positive habits, life passion, confidence building, mindfulness and simplicity.

As an entrepreneur, a mom of three and a homeowner, Barrie knows firsthand how valuable and life-changing it is to simplify, prioritize and organize your life and work in order to live your best life.

Made in the USA
San Bernardino, CA
03 October 2016